LELAND D. BLAND
Wright State University

SIGHT
SINGING
THROUGH
MELODIC
ANALYSIS

Burnham Inc., Publishers

Chicago

President: Kathleen Kusta
Vice-President: Brett J. Hallongren
General Manager: Richard Meade
Printer: Midland Press Corporation

Library of Congress Cataloging-in-Publication Data
Bland, Leland D.
   Sight singing through melodic analysis.

   1. Sight-singing.   2. Melodic analysis.   I. Title.
MT870.B58   1984   784.9'4   83–8184

ISBN 0-8304-1003-1 (cloth)
ISBN 0-88229-820-8 (paper)

Manufactured in the United States of America

10   9   8   7   6   5   4

 The paper used in this book meets the minimum requirements of American National Standard for Information Sciences—Permanence of Paper for Printed Library Materials, ANSI Z39.48-1984.

Homework
analysis

Contents

Preface

Any text intended for use in music theory courses on the college level must relate to the general purposes of theory and ear training instruction. Traditionally, a justification for the inclusion of theory and ear training in the college music curriculum has been that this instruction somehow improves musical performance and listening skills. As part of the ear training program, sight singing is the most available and direct means for applying melodic concepts to actual performance. *Sight Singing through Melodic Analysis* provides direct applications of analytical techniques to improving skill in sight singing. Although the book draws upon theoretical concepts, it is not a technical book, nor is it difficult to understand.

The word *analysis* has a broad but practical interpretation in this text. Even the earliest stages of the book involve simple but functional analysis as the basis for singing melodies at sight. Many of the melodies and exercises have a special format, based on Schenkerian analysis, which provides a guide for discovering and interpreting various structural levels in tonal melodies. Space is provided for written analyses of representative types of melodies. Given a tonal melody for analysis, students learn to (1) distinguish between structural and decorative tones within horizontal triad outlines, (2) recognize and interpret melodic shapes associated with triad outlines in various positions, and (3) recognize and interpret overall melodic shapes within entire phrases.

Material is arranged logically for developing an awareness of basic tonal relationships, phrases, and common shapes and motions in melodies. Rather than beginning with bits and pieces, such as individual intervals, the book progresses from general concepts to more specific ones. In the very first lesson, students deal with a slightly larger context than that of individual intervals: namely, horizontal outlines of the tonic triad. Since the sound of the tonic triad is familiar to everyone, students are able to grasp its outline as a basic context in melodies. Techniques of melodic embellishment are covered as the book progresses. Students learn to consider details in melodies in relation to larger patterns. Melodic contour is utilized frequently as a means for developing tonal memory. The melodies for sight singing, composed especially for the book, provide a maximum experience in each reading problem studied.

HOW TO USE THIS BOOK

Sight Singing through Melodic Analysis may be used independently, or it may be coordinated effectively with a number of theory texts or approaches during the first two years of music study in college. Aside from fundamentals, the use of this book requires no special background or training for either the student or the instructor.

Chapter 1, devoted entirely to discussion of rhythm and meter, contains extensive rhythmic drill. Sight singing begins in chapter 2 with the simplest relationships between time and pitch in melodies, and progresses to the more difficult melodies in later chapters. Most chapters contain (1) a short explanatory section, including a summary of new rhythmic material, (2) exercises in the melodic patterns to be studied, (3) melodic analysis, and (4) melodies for sight singing. New rhythms and meters are summarized at the point at which they are introduced; students are referred to the fuller explanations and rhythmic drills in chapter 1.

Although the material is designed to be taken in sequence from chapters 2 through 14, the order of some of the later chapters may be rearranged to suit individual needs.

CHAPTER 1

Rhythmic Organization in Music

All melodies in this book have underlying patterns of accent called *meter*. To understand meter in music, one may think of producing a series of pulsations with any sound source—singing, clapping, tapping on a drum or other object, or playing a musical instrument. If each pulse in a series is produced in an identical manner, no single pulse will stand out from the others. One of the standard units for representing the pulse, or beat, in music is the quarter note (♩). The quarter notes in example 1.1 represent a series of identical pulses. Any pulse in

Example 1.1

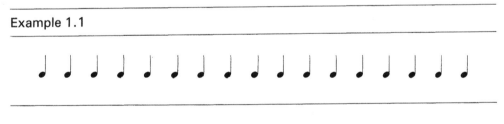

this series may be differentiated from the others if it is performed louder, or accented dynamically (>). The random placement of accents in example 1.2 pro-

Example 1.2

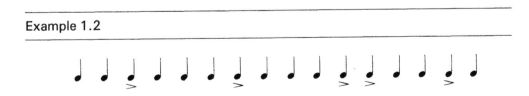

duces no particular metric grouping, while the regular pattern of accents in example 1.3 creates groups of two—one pulse accented and one unaccented. For ease in

Example 1.3

reading, bar lines may be drawn to separate the groupings into measures. In the pattern below, there are two beats per measure, or a meter in two.

Example 1.4

An accent on every third beat creates a meter in three.

Example 1.5

SIMPLE METERS

Since the first beat of each measure is normally performed with slightly more stress than the other beats, an accent sign is not necessary. The accent sign is usually reserved for indicating stress on normally unaccented beats or for giving extra stress to the accented beats. In example 1.6, the quarter note represents the beat for meters in two, three, and four. In a meter signature the top number designates the number of beats per measure, while the bottom number indicates the metric unit.

Example 1.6

An accent on every second beat creates a meter in two.

An accent on every third beat implies a meter in three.

An accent on every fourth beat indicates a meter in four; the third beat receives less accent than the first, but more than the second and fourth.

SIMPLE METERS. DUPLE DIVISION OF THE BEAT

All meters thus far have been simple meters. In simple meters the beats are often subdivided into two parts or multiples of two (duple division).

Example 1.7

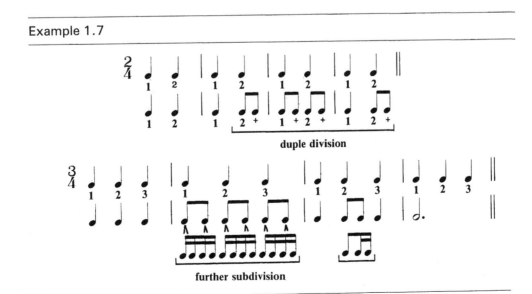

Units other than the quarter note are used frequently in music literature to represent the beat; meters such as ³/₈, ⁴/₂, and ³/₁₆ will be treated later in this chapter.

RHYTHM

Rhythm refers to duration of sound in the temporal dimension of music. Although rhythmic patterns may exist independently from metric groupings, the rhythms in this book are associated with specific meters. The durations of individual tones in rhythmic patterns may have various relationships with the unit of the beat in a particular meter:

1. A rhythmic pattern may contain durations that are equal to the value of the beat. In example 1.8, both the rhythm and the metric unit consist of quarter notes exclusively.

Example 1.8

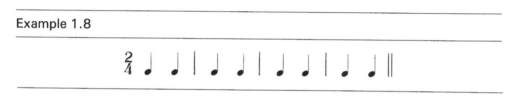

2. A rhythmic pattern may involve durations that are subdivisions of the beat.

Example 1.9

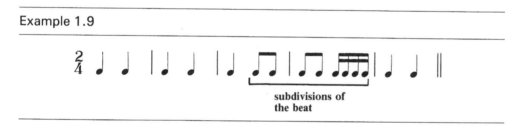

subdivisions of
the beat

3. A rhythmic pattern may contain durations that are greater than the beat.

Example 1.10

greater than
the beat

4. The rhythmic patterns in compositions are usually a mixture of the three possibilities above.

Example 1.11

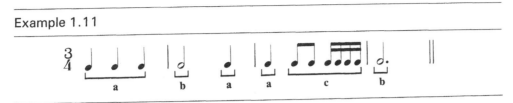

---

a. rhythmic duration equal to the beat
b. rhythmic duration greater than the beat
c. rhythmic duration less than the beat (subdivision)

Rhythmic Drill 1

The following exercises provide practice in reading rhythms in simple meters with two, three, or four beats per measure and duple division of the beat.

For the Greeks music & ruade not separate

Rhythmic Drill 2

Many compositions begin with only a portion of a measure. Before performing each of the following exercises, establish the meter by counting out the incomplete measure as a full measure.

Anacrusis (upbeat)

6/3/03

TIES

Note values may be combined by means of a *tie*—a slur between notes of the same pitch . The second note of the tie is not articulated, but its value is added to that of the first.

Rhythmic Drill 3

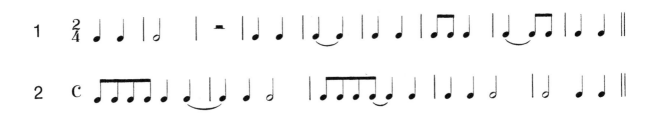

DOTTED NOTES

If the second note of a tie is equal to half the value of the first, then a dot may be used to replace the tie. The following example shows the relationship between tied and dotted notes.

Example 1.12

Rhythmic Drill 4

The following exercises contain dotted notes.

9 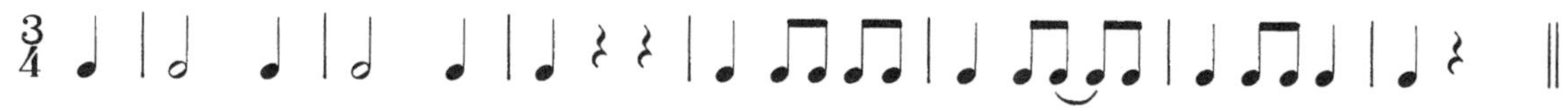

10 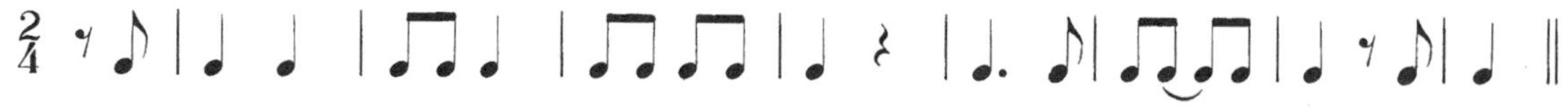

11 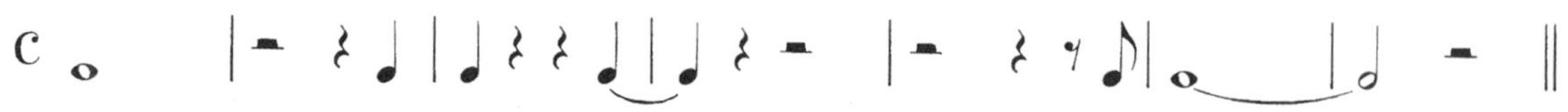

12 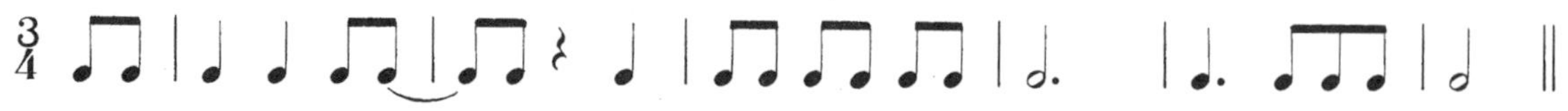

13 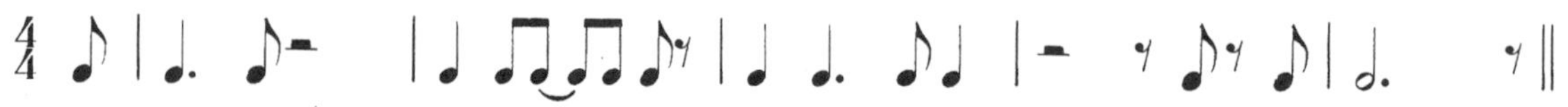

14 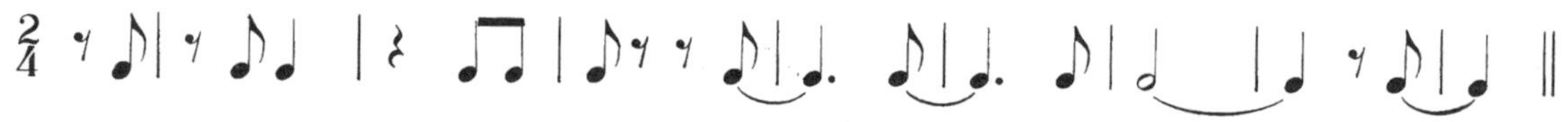

15 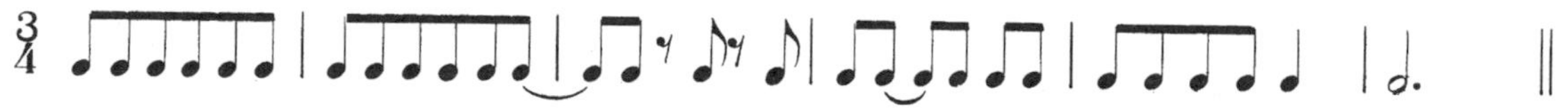

16 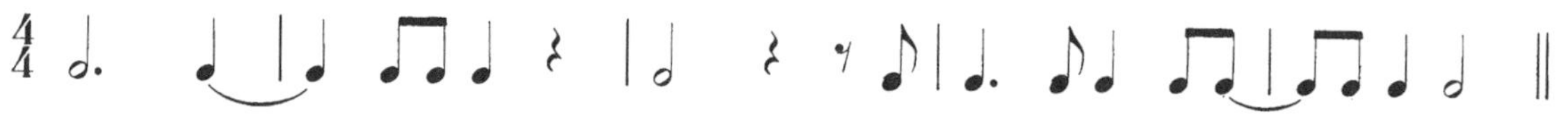

17 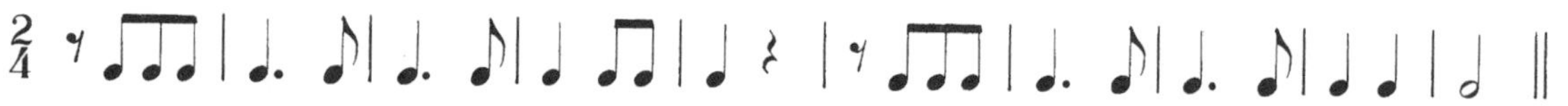

18 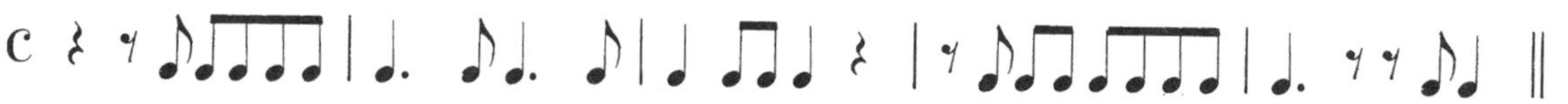

19 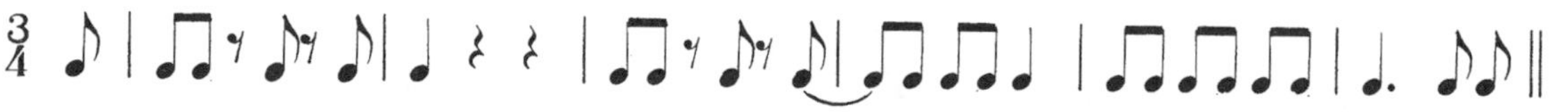

20 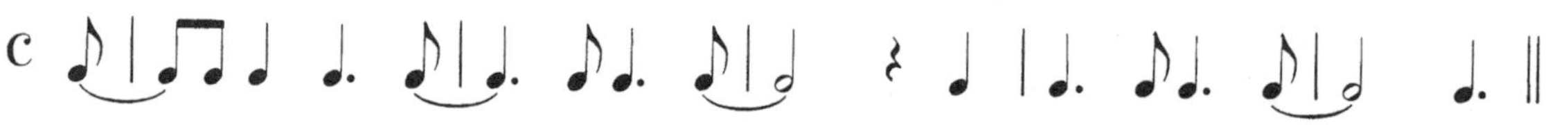

21 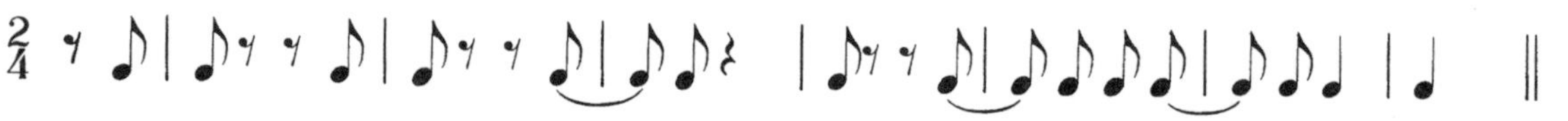

SIMPLE METERS. FURTHER SUBDIVISIONS OF THE BEAT

Table 1.1 demonstrates simple meters with subdivisions of the beat into 4.

Table 1.1. Simple meters.

Rhythmic Drill 5

The following exercises in simple meters contain subdivisions of the beat into four.

2 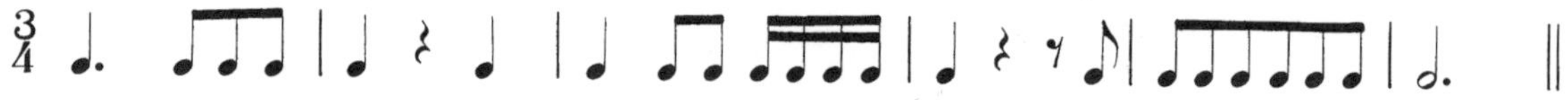

3 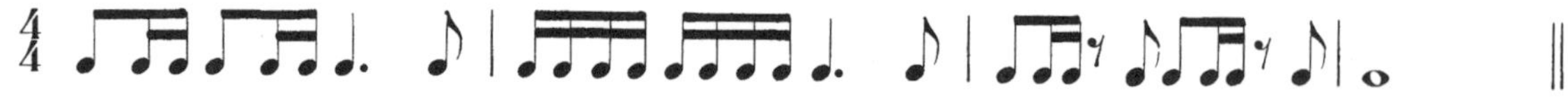

4 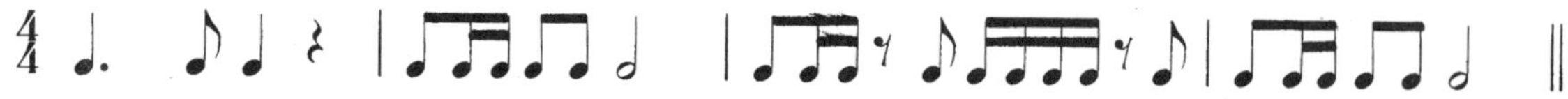

5 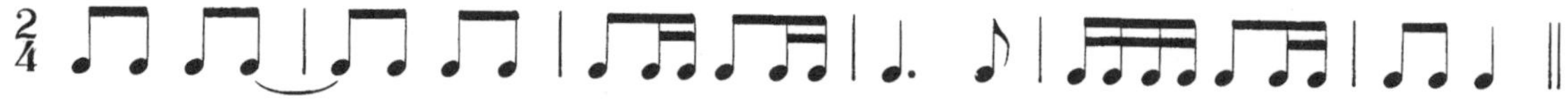

6 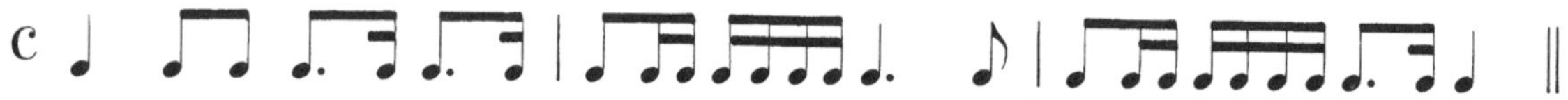

7 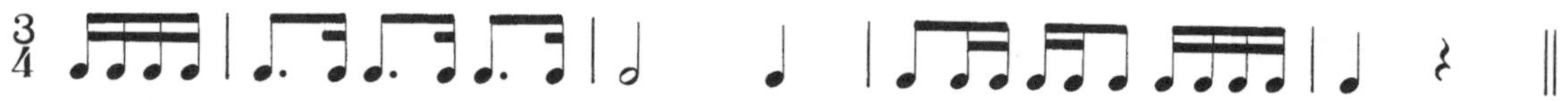

8 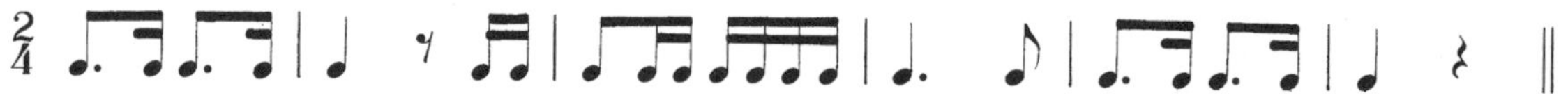

9 

10 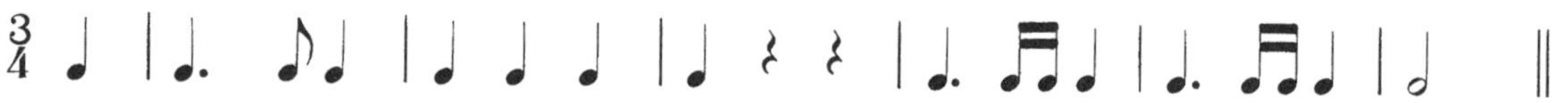

11 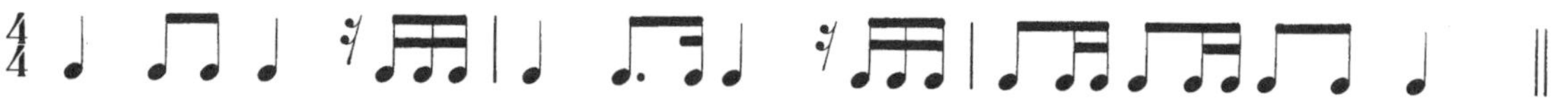

12 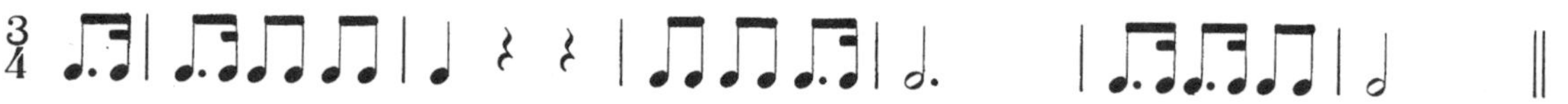

13 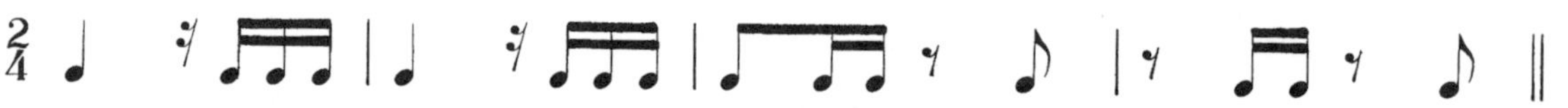

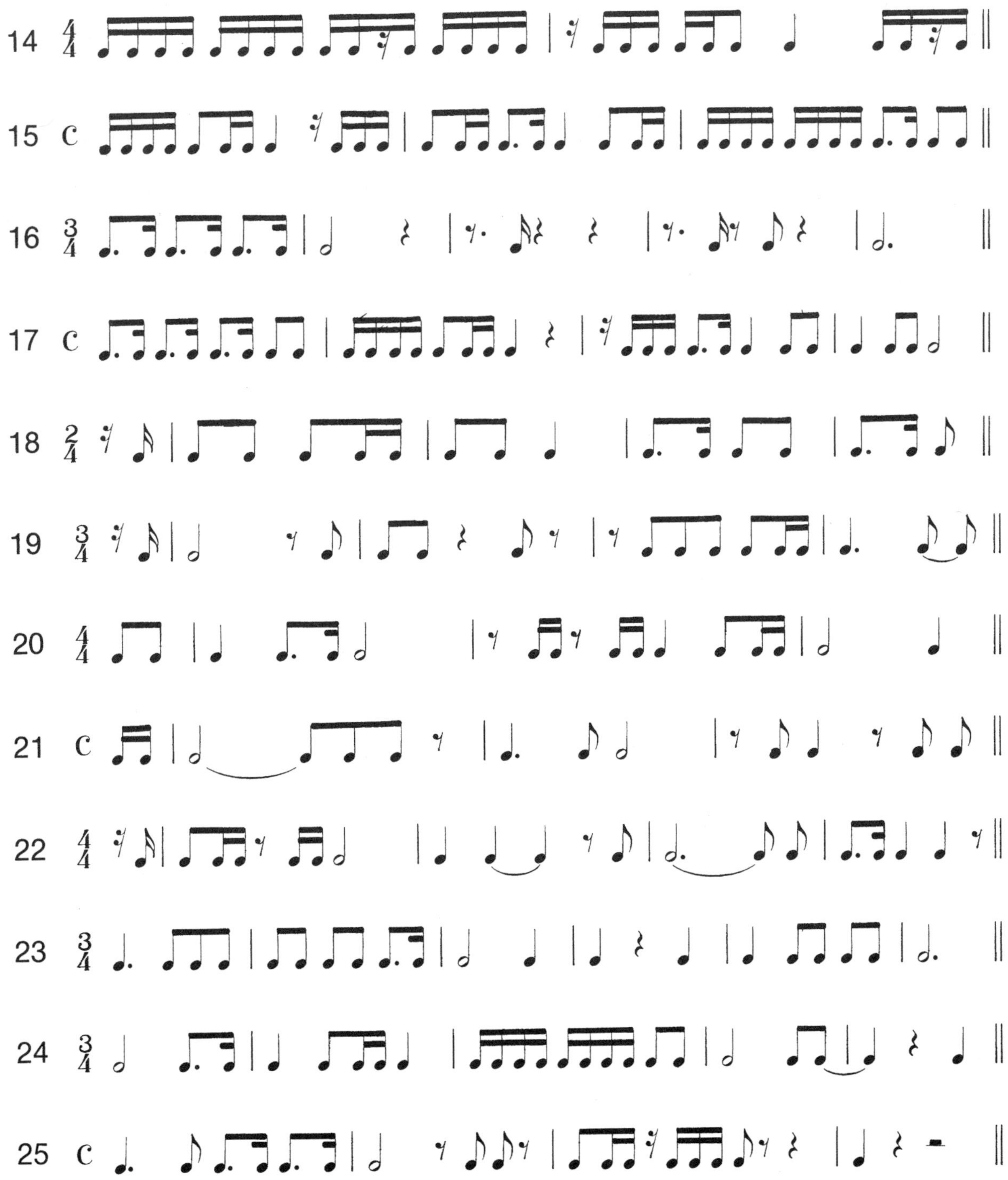
14
15
16
17
18
19
20
21
22
23
24
25

COMPOUND METERS

Meters in two, three, or four with triple subdivisions of the beat are called *compound meters*. In table 1.2, compare simple meters with compound meters in two, three, and four.

Table 1.2. Comparison of simple and compound meters.

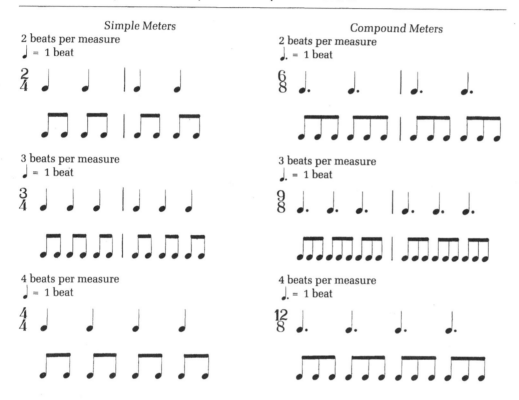

Rhythmic Drill 6

The following exercises are in compound meters.

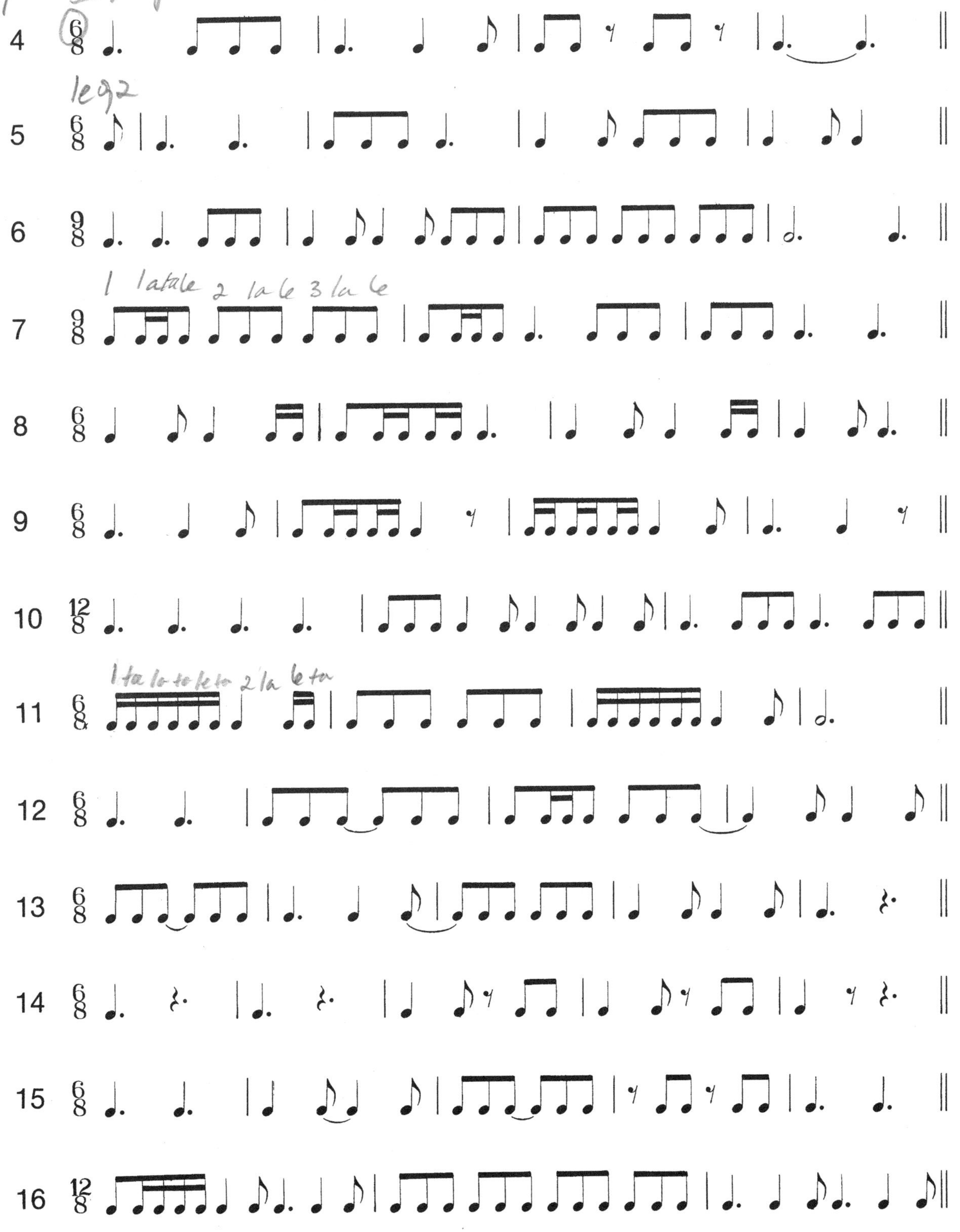

triple → 9/8   12/8 quadruple

compound duple

leg2

17 

18 

19 
1 ta l
3 la le

20 

21 

22 
1 la le 2 la le 3 la le

23 

24 

25 

26 

27 

Table 1.3. The dotted eighth note in 6/8 and 3/8 meters.

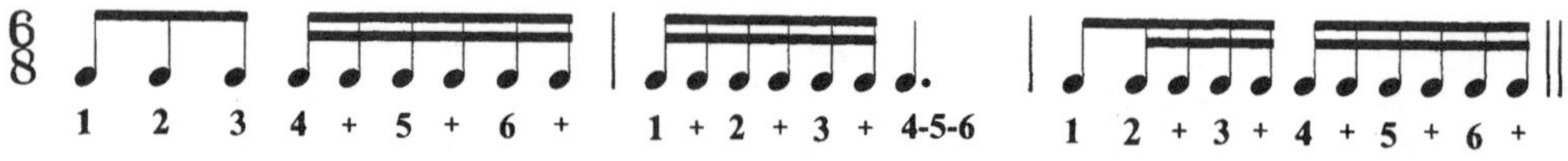
1 2 3 4 + 5 + 6 +
1 + 2 + 3 + 4-5-6
1 2 + 3 + 4 + 5 + 6 +

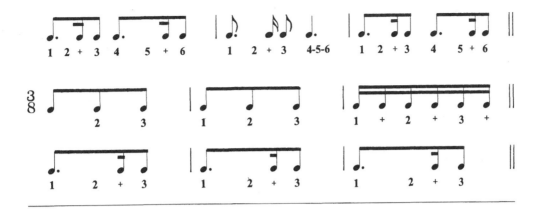

Numbers 28 through 53 contain dotted eighth notes.

28

29

30

31

32

33

34

35

36

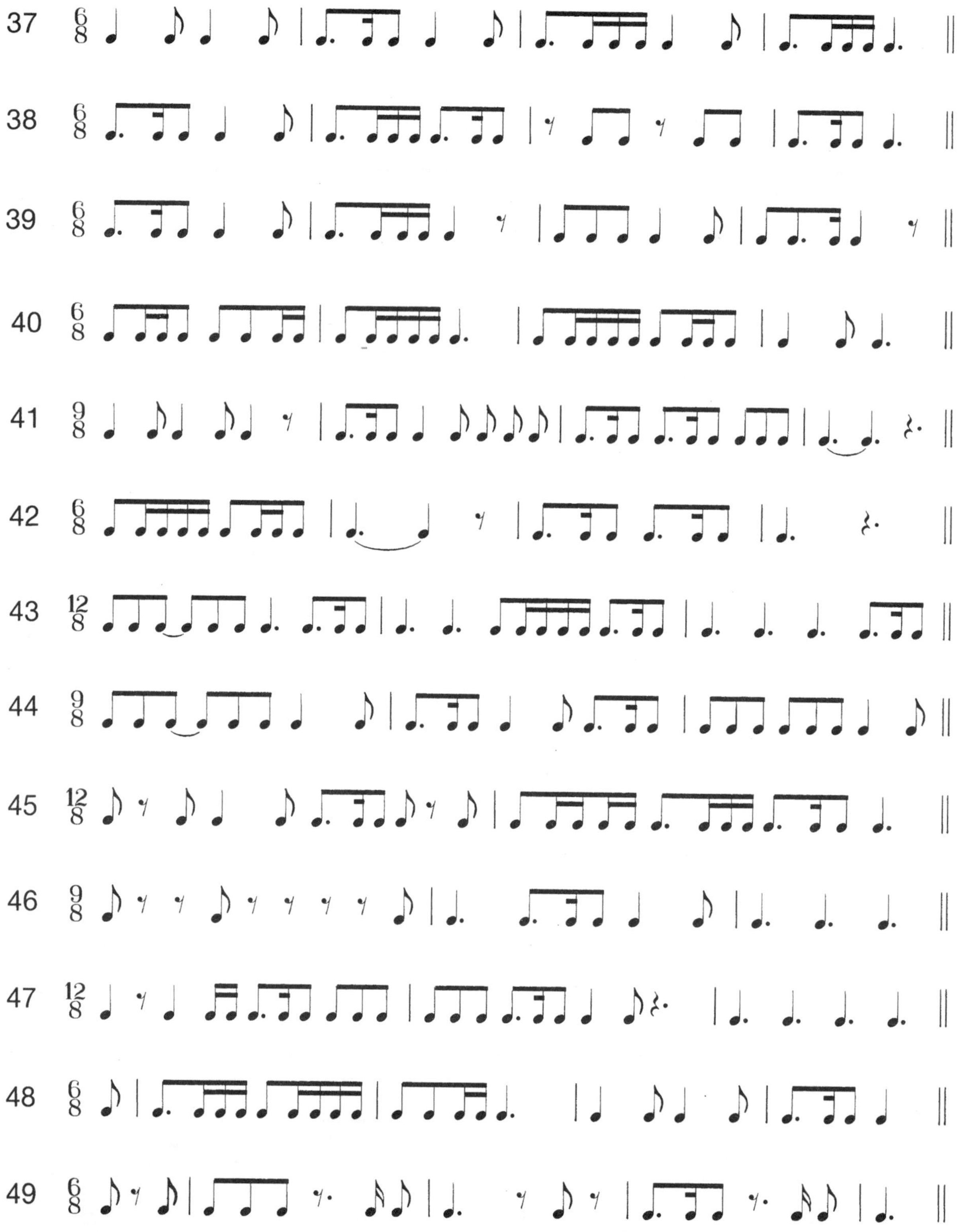
37
38
39
40
41
42
43
44
45
46
47
48
49

METERS IN ³/₈, ⁴/₈, ³/₁₆, AND ⁶/₁₆

Rhythmic Drill 7

REVIEW OF PREVIOUS MATERIAL

19

20

21

22

23

24

25

SYNCOPATION

As mentioned earlier, a particular meter is established through a recurring pattern of strong and weak beats. Any deviation from the established accent pattern of a meter is called *syncopation*. Three common means for shifting accents are: (1) stressing a weak beat dynamically, (2) connecting weak beats to succeeding beats, or (3) placing a rest on a strong beat. In the first way, as shown in example 1.13, the dynamic accent is shifted to the normally unaccented beat—in this case, the second beat. This shift of accent makes a very noticeable contrast to the expected pattern in 4/4 meter. Syncopation through dynamic accents is produced in

Example 1.13

meters in three by a shift of accent from the first beat to either or both of the second and third beats.

In the second means of shifting accents, a weak beat is connected to the succeeding beat or beats. In example 1.14, attention is drawn to the second beat because it is connected to the third beat.

Example 1.14

In example 1.15, the normally weak third beat is connected to the succeeding beat in the next measure.

Example 1.15

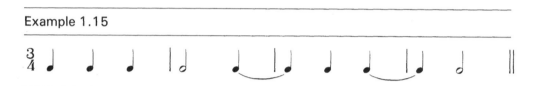

The third way of shifting accent is to place a rest on the strong beat, or at least on the first part of that beat (example 1.16).

Example 1.16

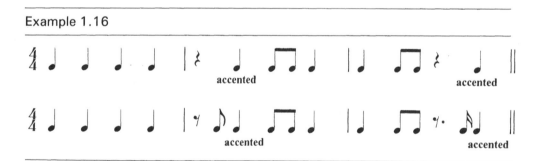

Rhythmic Drill 8

In the exercises below, dynamic accents on normally weak beats produce syncopation.

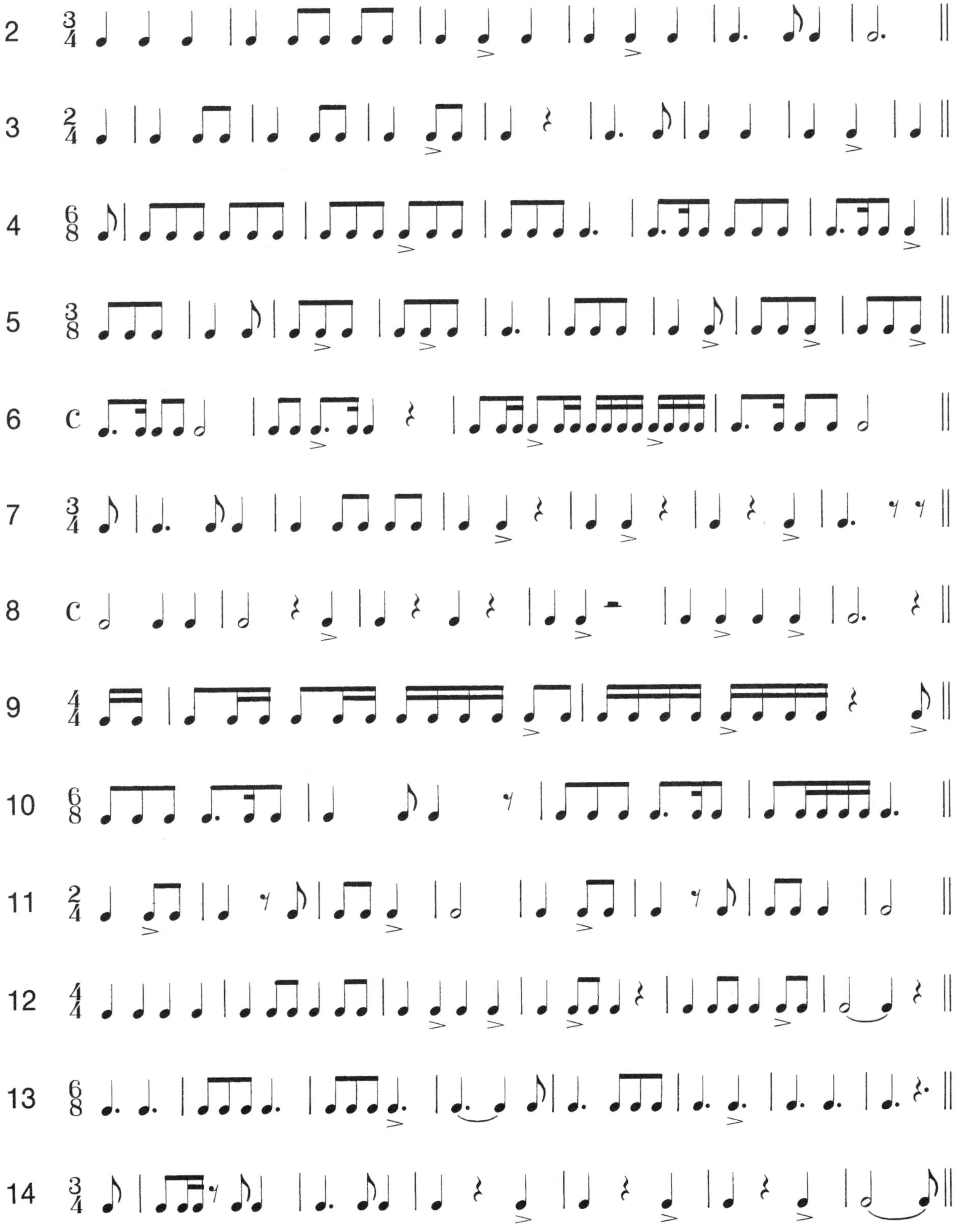
2
3
4
5
6
7
8
9
10
11
12
13
14

15

In the following exercises, syncopation is created by connecting weak beats to succeeding beats.

16

17

18

19

20

21

22

23

24

25

26

In the next exercises, syncopation is created by rests on strong beats.

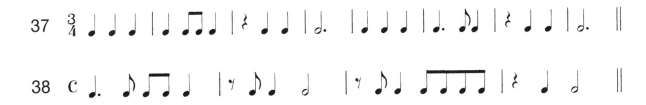

39 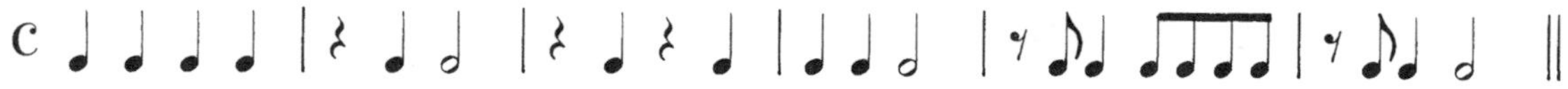

40 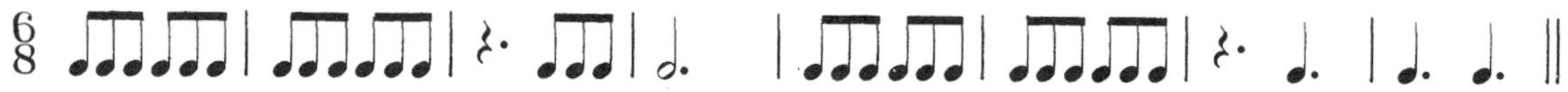

41 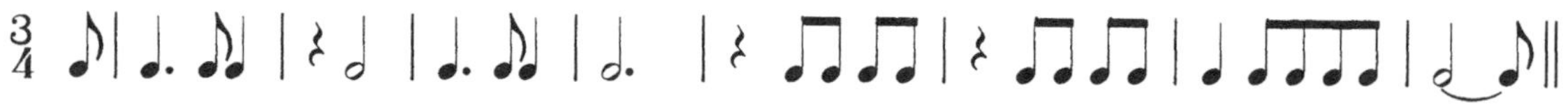

42 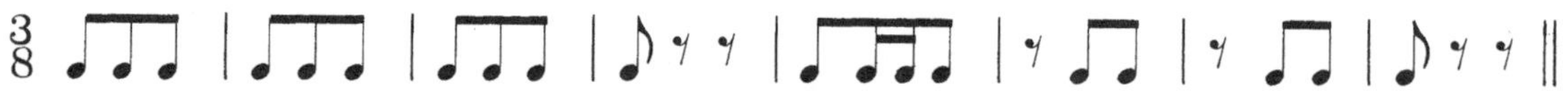

43 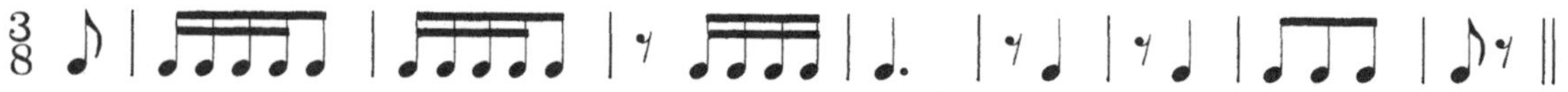

44 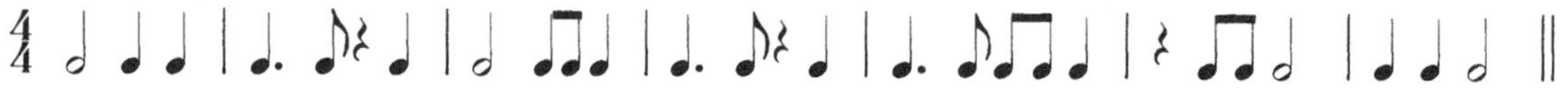

45 

46 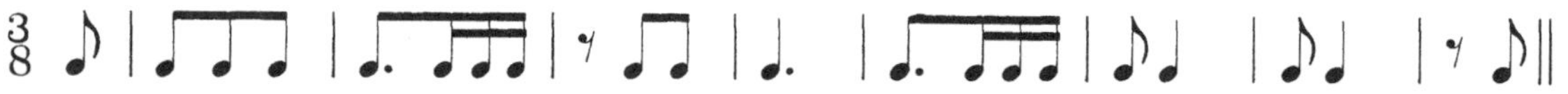

47 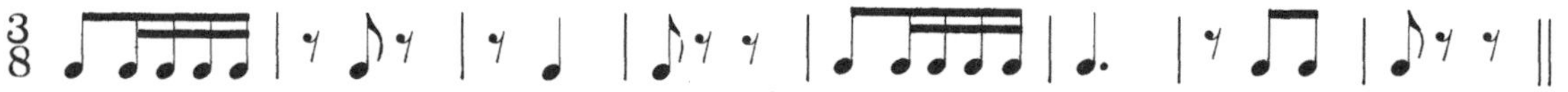

48 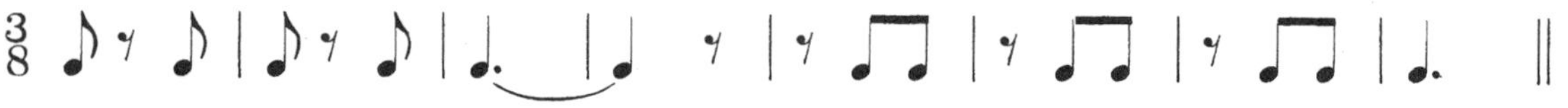

49 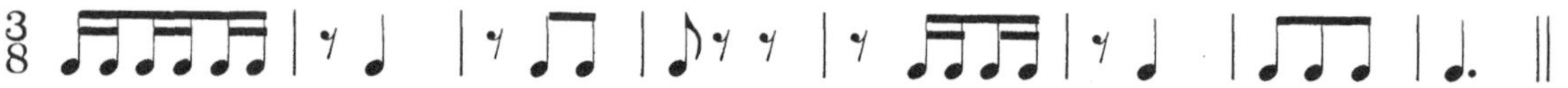

50 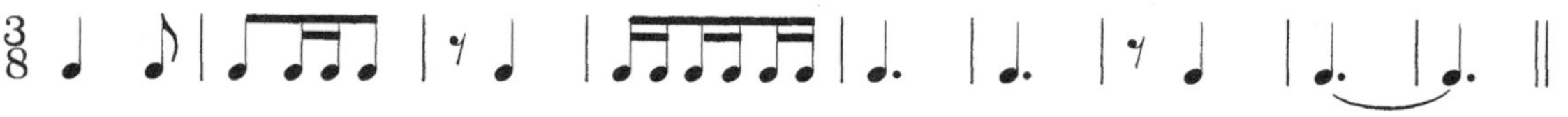

51 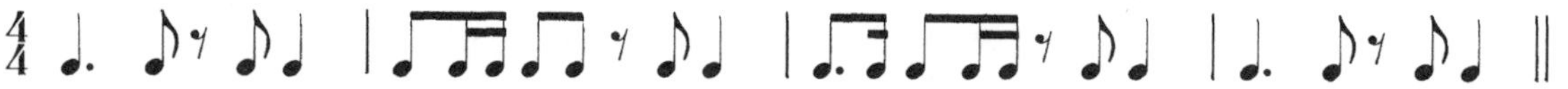

SYNCOPATION WITHIN THE BEAT

The initial portion of a beat is strong (say, the first of four sixteenth notes); a dynamic accent placed on any other subdivision produces syncopation within the beat (example 1.17).

Example 1.17

Syncopations are created in example 1.18 by ties between weak portions of the beat.

Example 1.18

In example 1.19, the second half of the first beat has more stress because it is tied to the succeeding beat.

Example 1.19

The beat in compound meters may be syncopated internally also (example 1.20).

Example 1.20

Rhythmic Drill 9

This exercise contains syncopation within the beat.

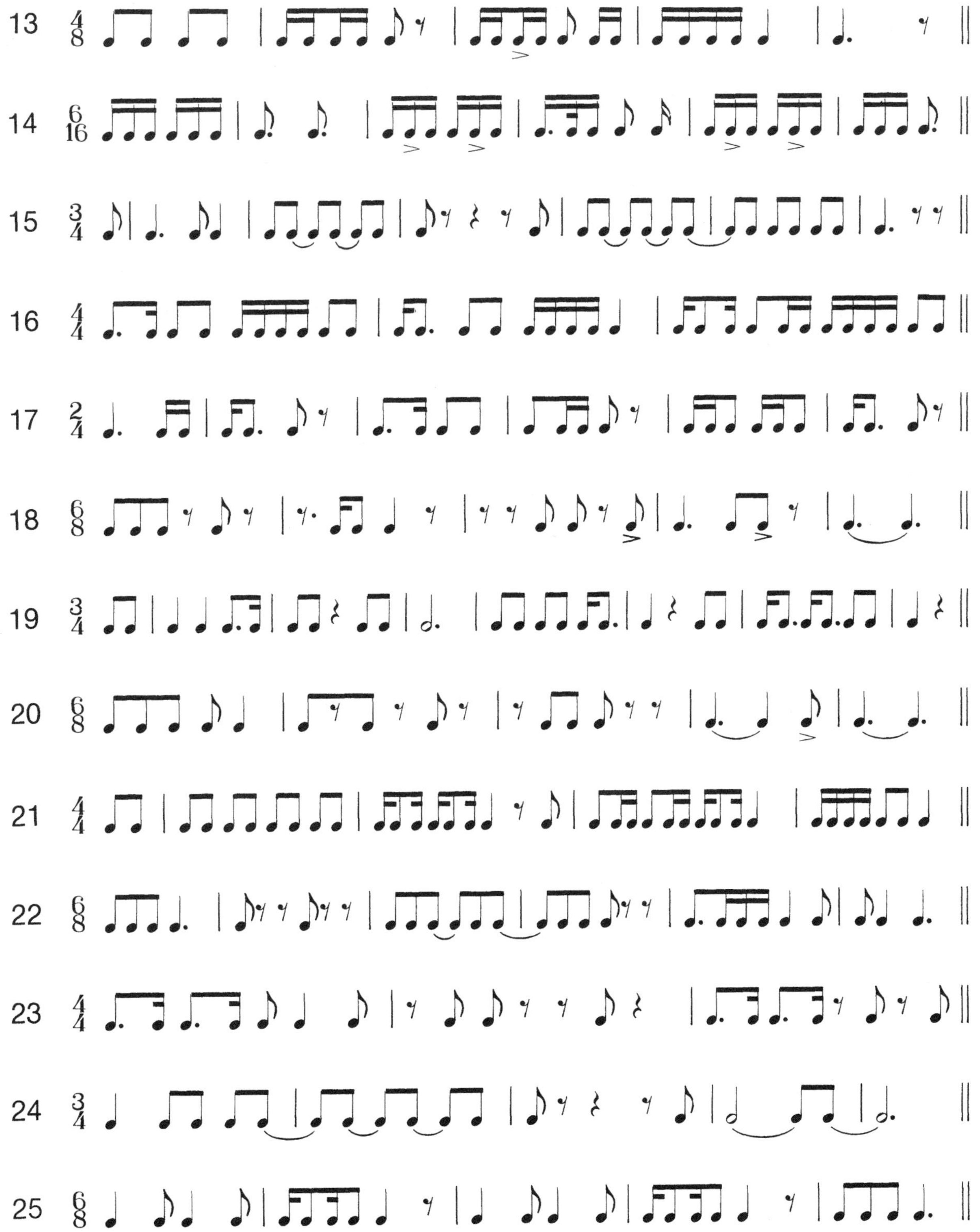
13
14
15
16
17
18
19
20
21
22
23
24
25

METERS IN 4/2, 3/2, 2/2, AND 6/4

Rhythmic Drill 10

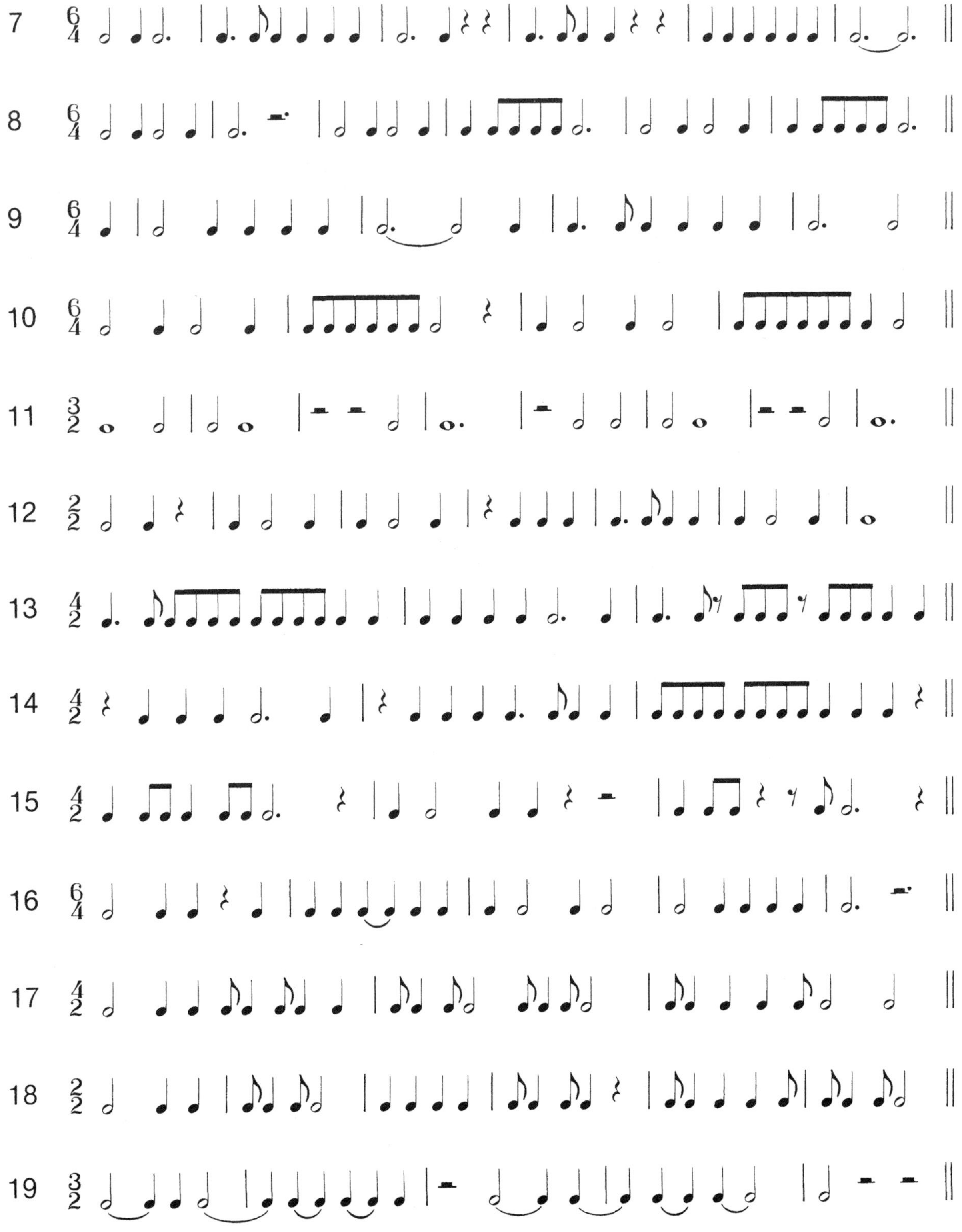
7
8
9
10
11
12
13
14
15
16
17
18
19

METERS WITH ASYMMETRICAL GROUPINGS

Meters such as ⁵/₄, ⁵/₈, and ⁷/₈ have asymmetrical accent patterns. Typical accent groupings are demonstrated in example 1.21.

Example 1.21

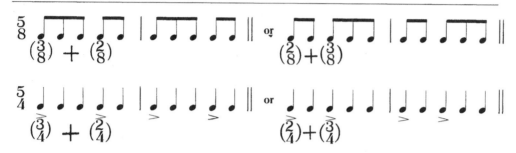

Some of the ways ⁷/₈ may be grouped are shown in example 1.22.

Example 1.22

Some meters may have either symmetrical or asymmetrical accent groupings. Example 1.23 demonstrates both symmetrical and asymmetrical groupings for ⁸/₈ and ¹⁰/₈ meters.

Example 1.23

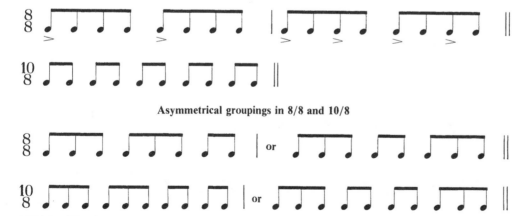

Rhythmic Drill 11

The following exercises contain asymmetrical groupings.

25 7/16
26 7/4
27 8/4
28 10/4
29 8/16
30 7/16
31 10/8
32 5/16
33 7/4
34 7/16
35 10/4
36 10/16
37 5/16

SIMPLE METERS WITH TRIPLE DIVISION OF THE BEAT

Beats with triple division (compound beats) may occur within simple meters, such as 2/4 or 4/4.

Rhythmic Drill 12

In the following exercises, some of the beats have triple division.

SIMPLE METERS WITH TRIPLE DIVISION WITHIN THE BEAT

Rhythmic Drill 13

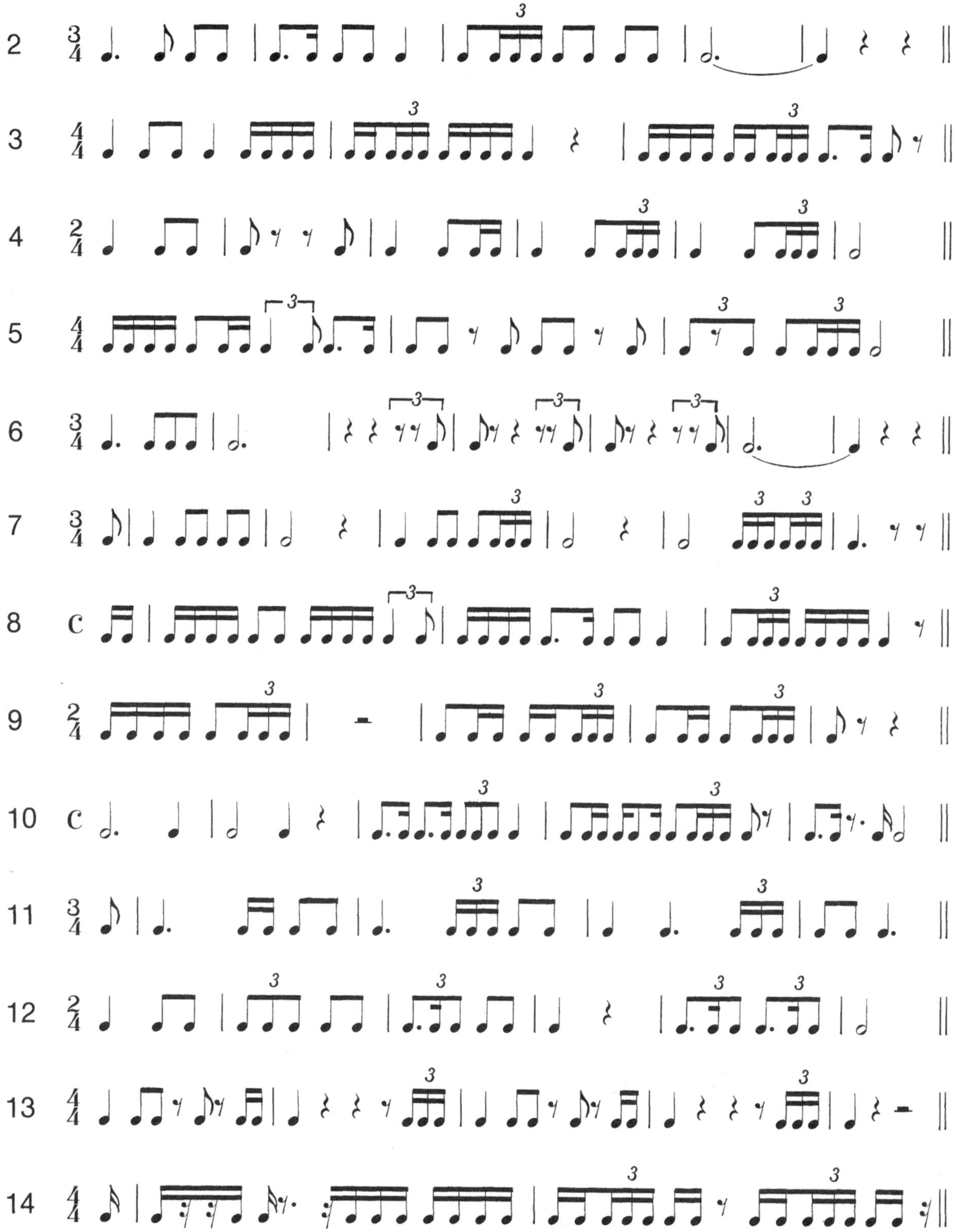
2
3
4
5
6
7
8
9
10
11
12
13
14

15

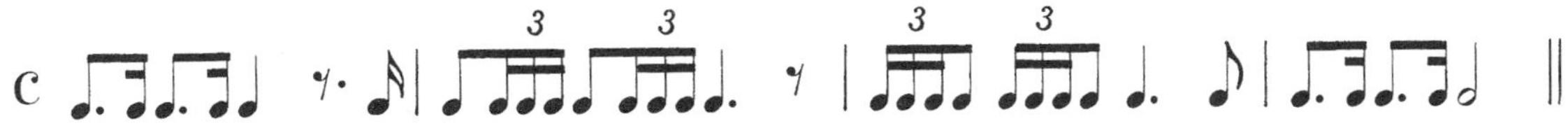

COMPOUND METERS WITH DUPLE DIVISION OF THE BEAT

In compound meters, characteristics of simple meters may be introduced if beats with duple divisions are interspersed with the compound beats.

Rhythmic Drill 14

MULTIBEAT DUPLETS AND TRIPLETS

The use of three notes to replace two notes of the same value, or the reverse, is not confined to divisions of individual beats. Such relationships may involve several beats—even an entire measure. In the patterns in example 1.24, triplets replace two beats and duplets replace three beats.

Example 1.24

Rhythmic Drill 15

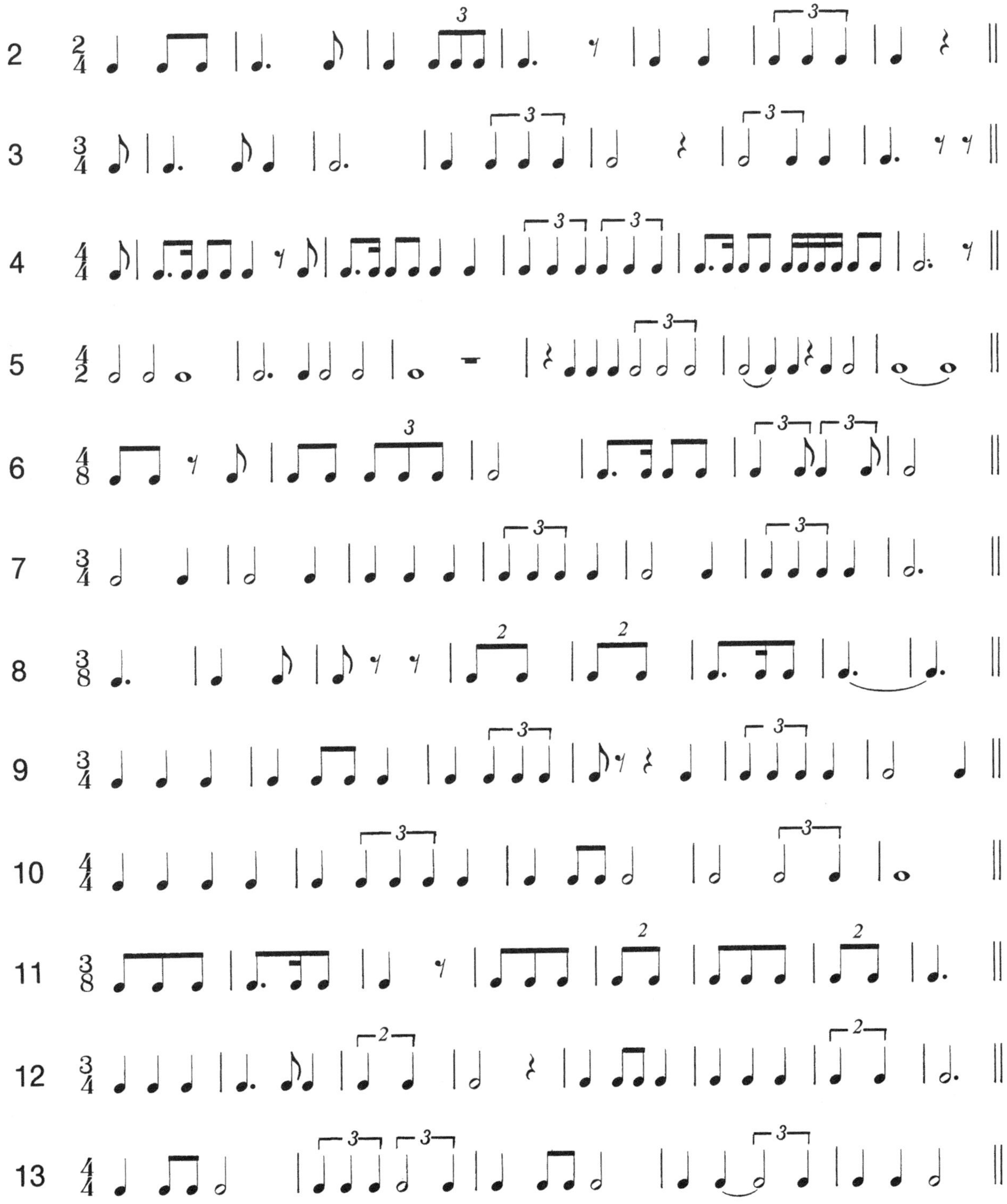
2
3
4
5
6
7
8
9
10
11
12
13

HEMIOLA AND OTHER SHIFTS OF ACCENT

A temporary shift of accent groupings from threes to twos within a prevailing meter is called a *hemiola*; no change of meter signature is required. Example 1.25 demonstrates typical cases of hemiola. As may be seen in rhythmic drill 16, other shifts of accent are possible as well.

Example 1.25

Rhythmic Drill 16

The following exercises contain hemiola and other shifts of accent.

CHANGING METERS

Rhythmic Drill 17

Meter changes may occur within a single composition. In numbers 1 through 9, the ♪ is the constant pulse unit throughout.

In numbers 10 through 14, the ♩ is the constant pulse unit throughout.

In some meter changes, relationships between the old and the new meters need clarification. In example 1.26, the meter changes from ³/₄ to ⁶/₈. The ♪ = ♪ above the meter change indicates that the ♪ in the *old* meter is the same in tempo and duration as the ♪ in the *new* meter.

Example 1.26

Although the rhythmic pattern and meter change in example 1.27 are identical to those in example 1.26, the units equated above the meter change are different. In example 1.27, the ♩. = ♩ indicates that the ♩. in ⁶/₈ meter is equal in tempo and duration to the ♩ in ³/₄ meter.

Example 1.27

Rhythmic Drill 18

The following exercises contain changes in meter.

13
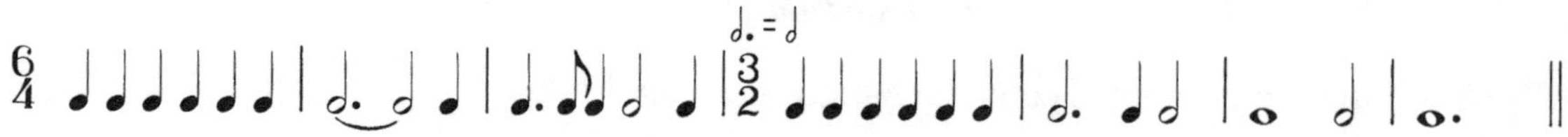

14
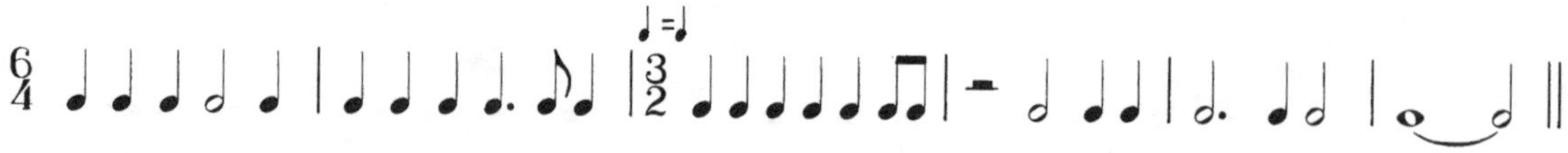

15
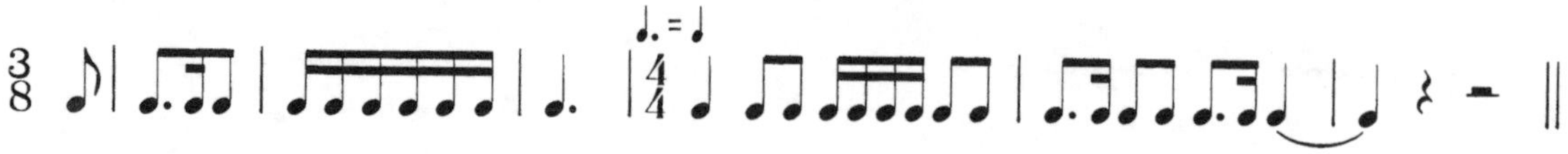

16
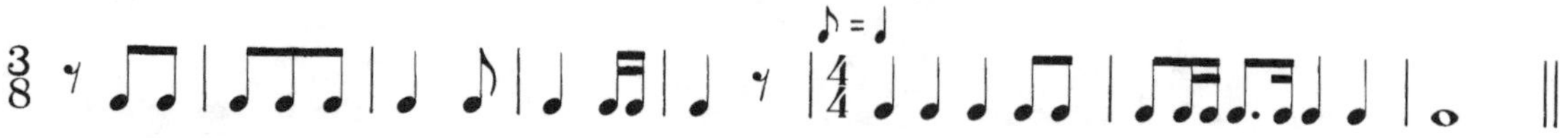

17
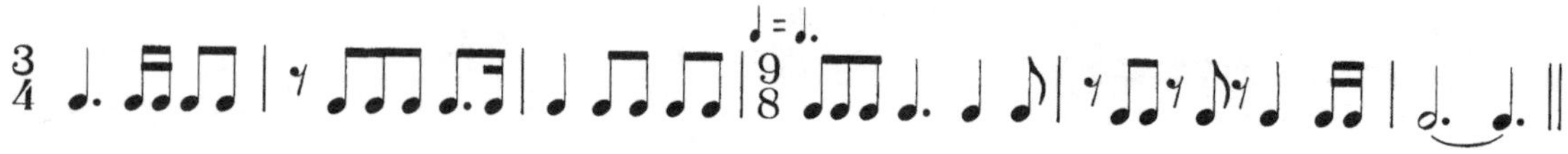

18
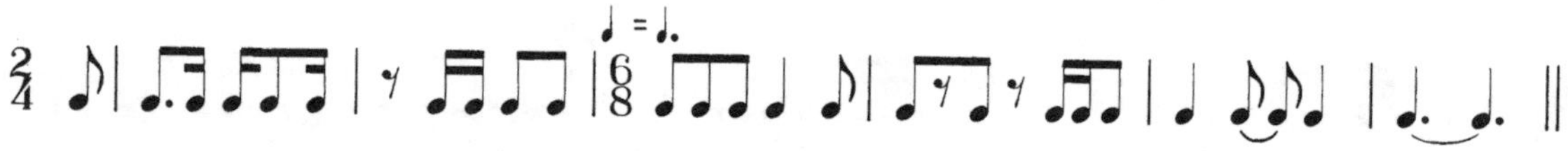

19
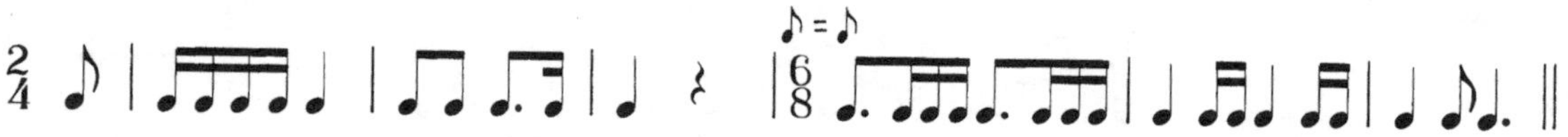

20
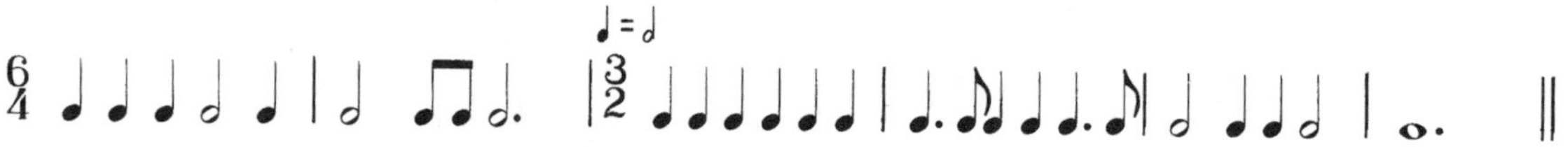

21
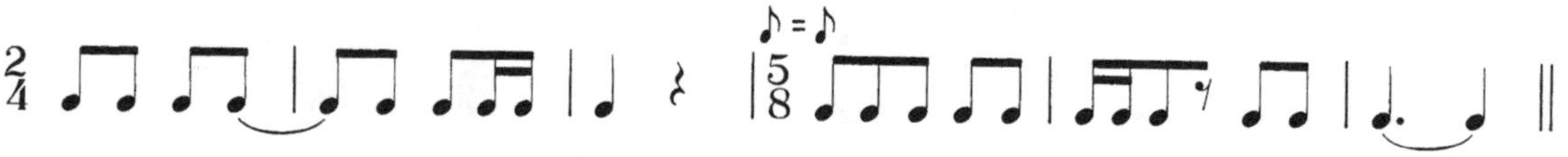

CHAPTER 2

Harmonic Outlines in Melodies:
The Tonic Triad

Tonal melodies are often organized around underlying harmonic outlines. Although all melodies contain individual pitches and intervals, analysis reveals that even seemingly complex tonal melodies often have simple horizontal outlines of harmonies prolonged in time through various ornamental devices.

The first, third, and fifth scale degrees of any key form the *tonic triad*. In example 2.1, the tonic triad in C major is notated harmonically, or vertically. The tones

Example 2.1

of a tonic triad may also be sounded and notated separately, or melodically (example 2.2).

Example 2.2

The top staff in example 2.3 has a melodic segment in the key of C major. The reduction* beneath demonstrates that the tonal material of this melody consists entirely of a horizontal outline of the tonic triad, or the first, third, and fifth scale degrees in the key of C major.

Example 2.3

Since an awareness of underlying harmonic outlines provides an indispensable background for reading tonal melodies, the tonic triad outline, rather than the individual intervals, will serve as the basic structural unit on which to build skill in sight singing. As an introduction to the techniques developed in this book, all melodies in this chapter have outlines of the tonic triad as their structural foundations.

Before beginning to sing melodies, it is wise to adopt some basic procedures for orientation. After the proper clef, key, and meter are determined, the pitch and rhythmic placement of the starting note must be established. Does the melody begin on the first, third, or other beat of the measure? Does it begin on a fraction of a beat? (See chapter 1, rhythmic drill 2.) In addition, a melody should be scanned for any overall characteristics that might give important clues to its performance; large leaps, overall contour or melodic shape, and underlying triad outlines should be taken into account.

As part of the preparation for sight singing any melody or exercise, the sound of the tonic triad should be well established in the ear. A special effort should be made to retain the tonic triad sound in the ear as the melody or exercise unfolds. Special techniques for scanning melodies for discovering relationships between tones will be developed as the study progresses.

All melodies in this chapter are written in either the treble or bass clef. Meters are either 2/4, 3/4, or 4/4. Starting pitches are the first, third, or fifth of the tonic triad. In fact, tonal material in the beginning melodies will be limited to tonic triad outlines.

---

*The notation in the reductions in this book is adapted from analytical techniques associated with Heinrich Schenker. Open notes indicate harmonic tones. Beginning with the section on passing tones, closed notes will designate nonharmonic tones, or embellishing tones.

Exercise 1

The following tonic triad outlines are presented in several keys. Remember to establish the tonic triad outline in the ear before singing each line.

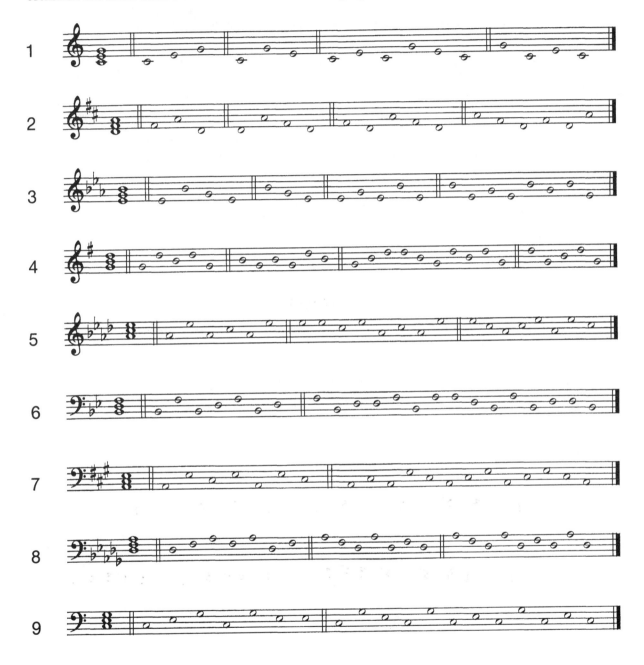

RHYTHMIC MATERIAL

Melodies in this chapter involve duple or triple meter, with duple divisions of the beat. Refer to the discussions of meter and rhythm in chapter 1. Typical rhythmic patterns are summarized below:

Extra drill in these patterns is found in chapter 1, rhythmic drills 1, 2, 3, and 4.

 **Melodies** 13/2/03

The following melodies are based on the tonic triad. The meters are duple or triple, with duple divisions of the beat.

PASSING TONES

Few melodies in music literature are limited to triad tones exclusively; most have embellishing tones which elaborate the basic harmonic outlines. One of the most common embellishing tones is the *passing tone*. In example 2.4, passing tones fill the spaces between tones of the triad outlines. The reduction beneath the melody distinguishes between triad tones and passing tones.

Example 2.4

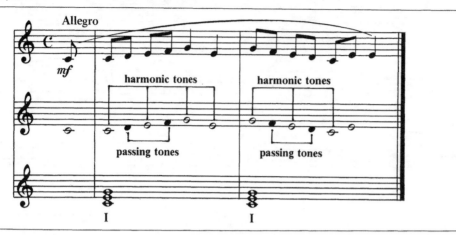

Hereafter, triad tones, or harmonic tones, will be referred to as *structural tones;* other tones will be called *embellishing tones* or *decorative tones.* With stepwise motion produced by passing tones, the possibilities for variety and interest in melodies are greatly increased.

Exercise 2

The following patterns contain tonic triad outlines with passing tones.

Melodies

The following melodies contain tonic triad outlines with passing tones. In melodies 13 through 16, a reduction beneath distinguishes between structural tones and passing tones. If any melody causes a problem in performance, sing the reduction first.

In numbers 17 through 22, make a reduction beneath each melody. Use the reductions as guides for singing the melodies.

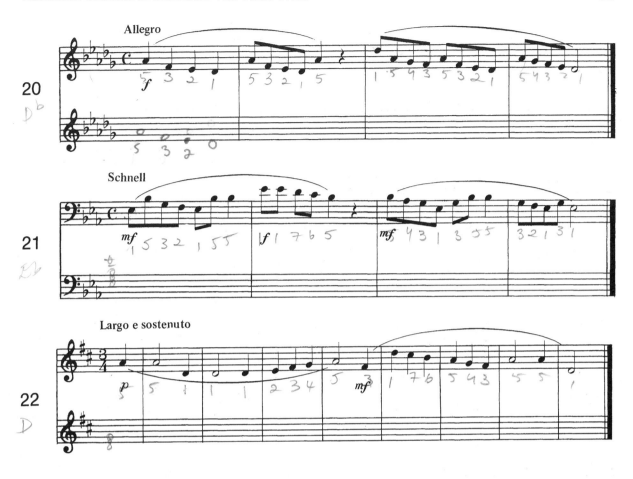

Exercise 3

In this exercise, triad outlines begin on either the third or fifth of the tonic triad.

INVERSIONS OF THE TONIC TRIAD OUTLINE

All harmonic outlines up to this point have involved the tonic triad in fundamental position. Triads may be inverted—rearranged so that the three tones are in different orders. Example 2.5 demonstrates the tonic triad arranged vertically in its three possible positions.

Example 2.5

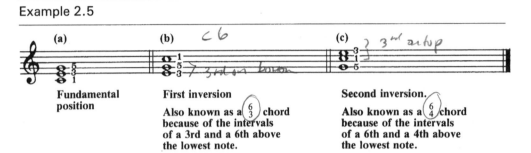

(a)   **(b)**   **(c)**

Fundamental position

First inversion

Also known as a $\binom{6}{3}$ chord because of the intervals of a 3rd and a 6th above the lowest note.

Second inversion.

Also known as a $\binom{6}{4}$ chord because of the intervals of a 6th and a 4th above the lowest note.

The tonic six-four outline is found in many melodies. Note the relationship between the fundamental position and the six-four position of the tonic triad in example 2.6.

Example 2.6

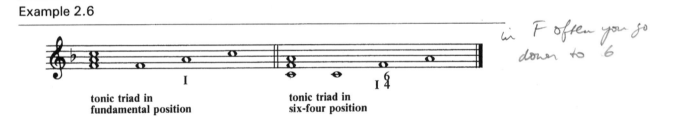

tonic triad in fundamental position

I

tonic triad in six-four position

I $\frac{6}{4}$

Although these two configurations are both outlines of the tonic triad, they have significant differences with regard to contour, or shape, in melodic lines. In example 2.7, the lines drawn over the triad outlines indicate shapes, or contours. Compare the contours of outlines of tonic triads in the fundamental position with those in the six-four position.

Example 2.7

triad contours in fundamental position

I

triad contours in six-four position

I $\frac{6}{4}$

Notice that the six-four outlines involve a larger distance between lower and upper notes. It must be understood that in this book ''triad outline'' and ''harmonic outline'' do not necessarily imply individual chords that may be used in harmonizing a melody. Rather, ''triad outline'' refers to the linear or horizontal aspect of a melody on a more general level.

Passing tones have the same relationships with structural tones regardless of the triad position. In example 2.8, outlines of the six-four triad contain passing tones.

Example 2.8

The six-four and six-three triad outlines each contain the interval of a fourth. To fill that interval, two passing tones may be needed (example 2.9).

Example 2.9

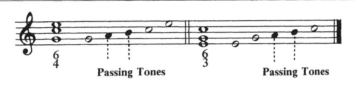

Exercise 4

This exercise contains outlines of the tonic triad in six-three and six-four positions with passing tones. Concentrate on each pattern as triad outlines with embellishments rather than as a series of intervals.

The following triad outlines are in six-four position and contain passing tones.

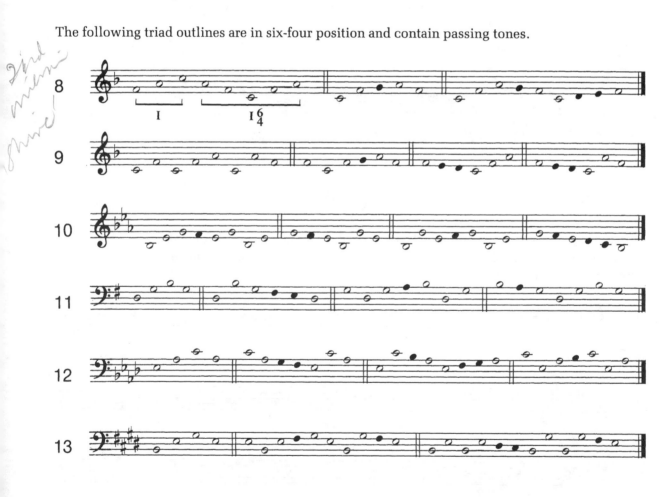

Melodies

The following melodies contain outlines of tonic triads in six-four position.
Passing tones are included.

In numbers 25 through 27, make reductions and sing.

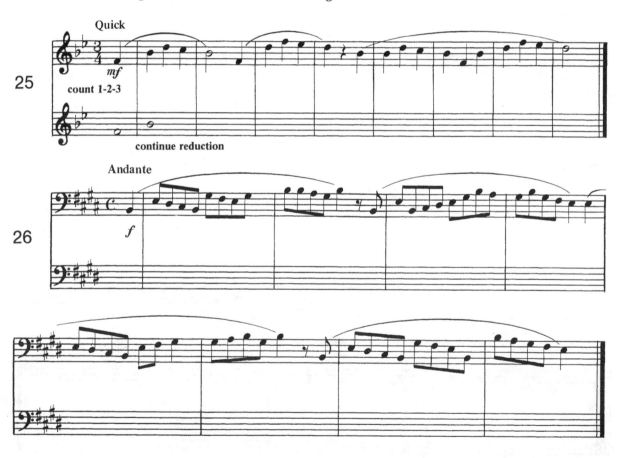

April 3/03

27

NEIGHBOR TONES

The *neighbor tone* differs fundamentally from the passing tone. While the passing tone is found between two structural tones of different pitch, the neighbor tone occurs between structural tones of the same pitch. In example 2.10, the pitches F and A serve as neighbor tones, respectively. Since neighbor tones may be above or below the decorated tone, the terms *upper* or *lower* neighbor often refer to these embellishments.

neighbouring
EX

1 2 1 7 1
3 4 3 2 3
5 6 5 4 5

Example 2.10

For further clarification of the function of neighbor tones, compare examples 2.11 and 2.12. In 2.11, the note C gets two beats; in 2.12, it is embellished by its neighbor tone, D. While adding melodic activity, the neighbor tone does not destroy the basic feeling of the note C in the final two beats of the measure.

Example 2.11

Example 2.12

2 beats

Examples 2.13 and 2.14 demonstrate the fundamentally different functions of passing tones and neighbor tones.

Example 2.13

Passing Tones

Passing tones provide a heightened sense of direction between structural tones.

Example 2.14

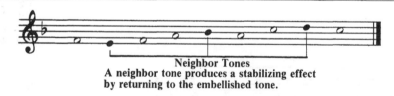

Neighbor Tones
A neighbor tone produces a stabilizing effect by returning to the embellished tone.

Exercise 5

This exercise contains triad outlines in various positions. Both passing tones and neighbor tones are included.

1/5/03

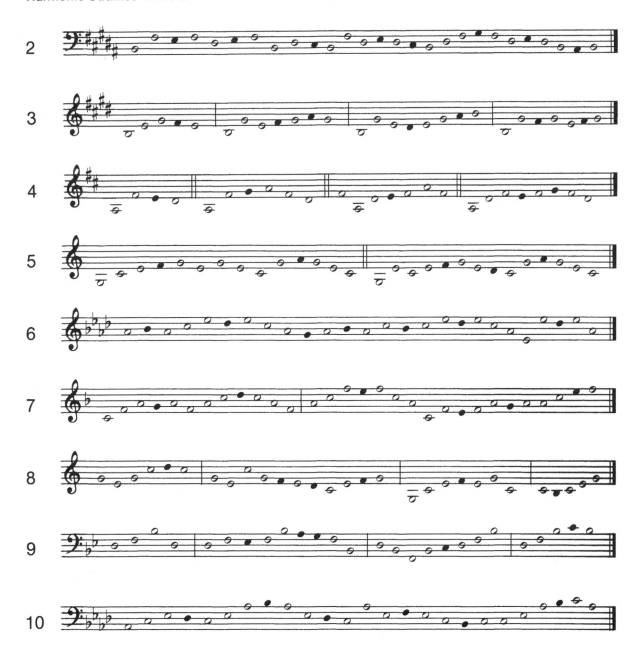

Exercise 6

This exercise has several series of pitches containing structural tones (harmonic tones) and embellishing tones. Make a reduction on each staff provided below. After completing each analysis, sing the pitches.

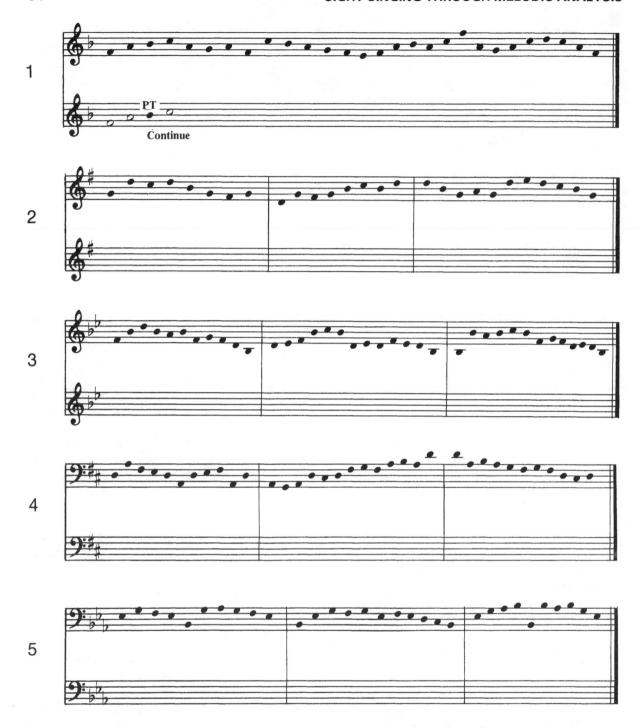

Melodies

The following melodies contain triad outlines in all positions. Both passing tones and neighbor tones are included. The dotted quarter note is introduced. (See chapter 1, rhythmic drills 3 and 4.)

APPOGGIATURAS

Although it is beyond the scope of this book to pursue all ramifications of the term *appoggiatura*, the following characteristics will suffice for analysis of the sight singing melodies: (1) An appoggiatura results from a melodic leap to the neighbor tone either above or below a structural tone, and (2) it usually occurs on an accented pulse and resolves to a structural tone on the last half of the pulse or on the next unaccented pulse. However, for the purpose of scanning melodies for underlying harmonic outlines, attention will be focused upon the structural tone to which an appoggiatura resolves rather than upon accent.

Structural tones in example 2.15 involve the D major triad. The appoggiatura (the pitch B) results from a leap to the upper neighbor of the note A, the fifth of the D major triad. In singing example 2.15, it may be beneficial to think of the appoggiatura as a whole step above the fifth of the D major triad, rather than as the interval of a sixth above the preceding note D. Before singing example 2.16, think of the appoggiatura as a half step above the structural tone B of the G major triad outline.

Example 2.15

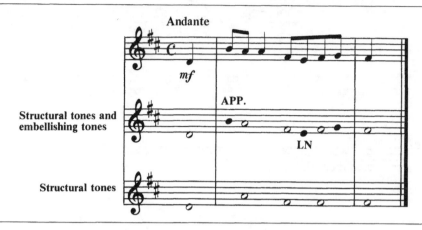

Example 2.16

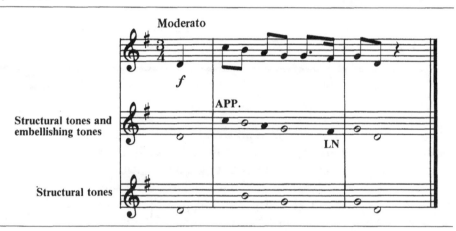

In example 2.17, consider the appoggiatura on the tone D as the lower neighbor of the structural tone E-flat, rather than as a minor sixth below the preceding B-flat. The appoggiatura on C in the last measure may be thought of as a step above the structural tone B-flat rather than as a fourth above the preceding G. Also study the appoggiaturas in example 2.18.

Example 2.17

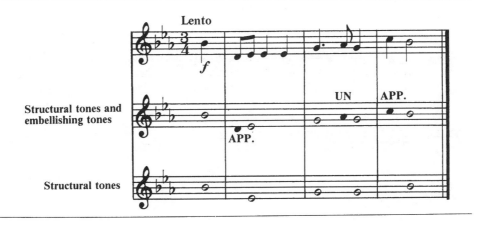

Example 2.18

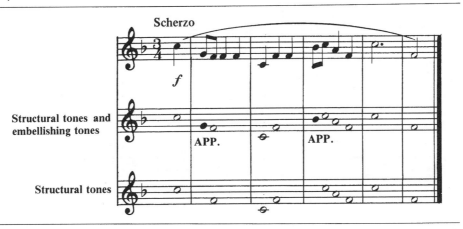

Exercise 7

This exercise contains tonic triad outlines in all positions. Passing tones, neighbor tones, and appoggiaturas are included.

Melodies

The following melodies contain outlines of the tonic triad, passing tones, neighbor tones, and appoggiaturas. If difficulties arise in singing any of the melodies, make reductions on a separate sheet of manuscript paper.

CHAPTER 3

Melodies Outlining the I and V Triads

Melodies in chapter 2 were based on outlines of the tonic triad. In this chapter, melodies will outline both the tonic (I) and dominant (V) triads. Adapting V triad outlines into that which has already been learned will be smooth because of two strong relationships: (1) The fifth scale degree is common to both triads, and (2) the V triad contains the seventh scale degree, or *leading tone*, which has a tendency to pull toward the tonic (see example 3.1). As a common tone, the fifth scale degree serves as an important structural link between outlines

Example 3.1

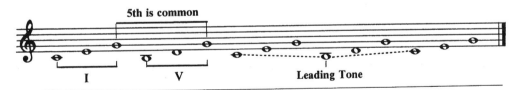

of I and V triads.

Although the fifth, seventh, and second scale degrees in melodies may be harmonized vertically with the V triad, the mere appearance of any of these tones does not necessarily imply the linear V triad outline. In example 3.2, the fifth scale degree and the leading tone appear consecutively but are clearly within the context of the tonic triad outline.

Example 3.2

No definite rule exists for deciding whether or not a V triad outline is implied in a particular melody. However, some general guidelines may be helpful. If the tones of the V triad occur only infrequently, perhaps they are best treated as embellishing tones to the tonic triad. For sight singing purposes, it is always best to consider the overall linear aspects of a melody and retain the tonic triad outline in the ear as much as possible. If the tones of the V triad are prominent in a melody, they may acquire the status of a structural chord outline. Example 3.3 demonstrates that a nearly identical set of pitches, enclosed in brackets, may function as embellishing tones to the tonic triad (a), or as an outline of the V⁶ (first inversion) triad (b).

Example 3.3

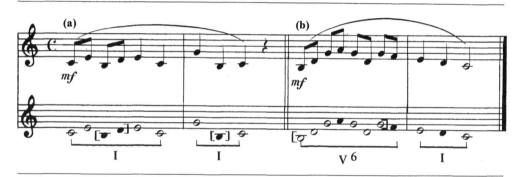

Exercise 8

Various combinations of I and V triad outlines are summarized in this exercise. Numbers 1 through 6 feature the fifth scale degree as a pivot tone; observe appearances of the leading tone as well.

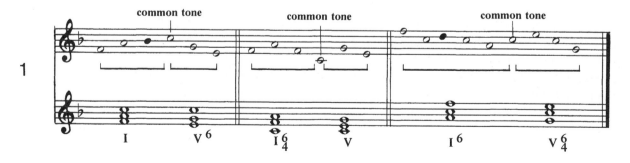

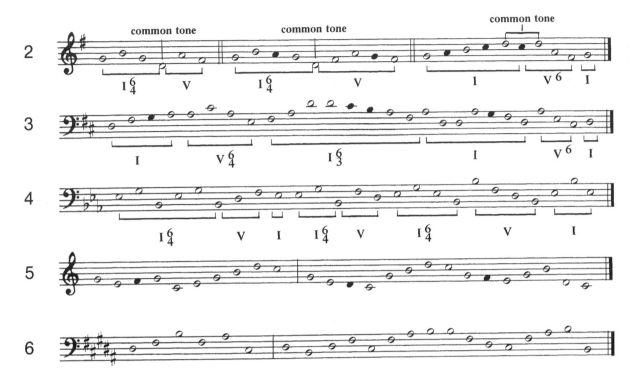

Numbers 7 through 12 emphasize the leading tone and its resolution.

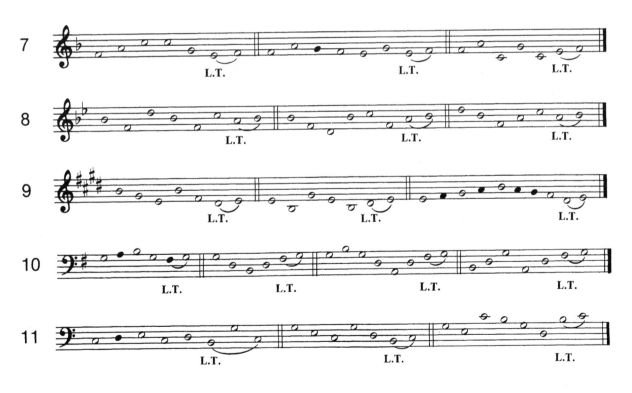

12   L.T.   L.T.   L.T.

NEW RHYTHMIC MATERIAL

Typical new rhythmic patterns are summarized below:

An additional drill in the above rhythmic patterns is found in chapter 1, rhythmic drill 6.

Melodies

In the following melodies, the fifth scale degree may act as a pivot tone between I and V triad outlines; observe resolutions of the leading tone. Space is provided for reductions beneath numbers 53 through 55. Make further reductions on separate manuscript paper as needed.

53

DELAY OF THE LEADING-TONE RESOLUTION

Motion from the leading tone to the tonic may be delayed by a prolongation of the leading tone. In the top staff of example 3.4, the leading tone, B, is prolonged

Example 3.4

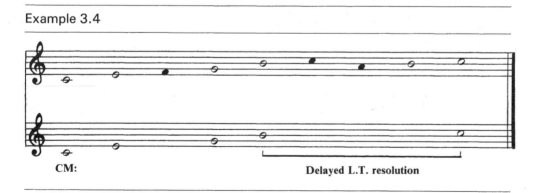

CM: Delayed L.T. resolution

by neighbor tones, causing a delay in its progression to the tonic. Such delays and elaborations may be so extensive that basic progressions from leading tone to the tonic are obscured. The series of pitches in the top staff of example 3.5 may not appear at first to have any structural implications. The reduction beneath, however, reveals that this passage is actually composed of two structural levels: (a) an overall motion from leading tone to the tonic, and (b) an elaboration of the tone G. When one sings a passage such as the one in example 3.5, the underlying sound of (a) should be remembered while singing the intervening tones of (b). Skill in re-

Example 3.5

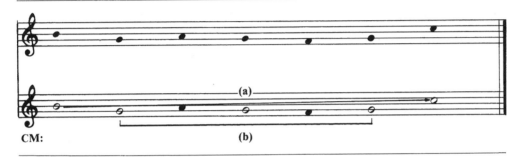

CM:

taining certain tones in the ear while singing others—or tonal memory—is essential when dealing with more than one structural level in melodies.

The delaying of melodic motions and tonal resolutions is an important form-building technique in musical composition. In fact, a delay in well-established motions, such as the one from the leading tone to the tonic, actually intensifies the expectation of an eventual resolution.

Exercise 9

The following harmonic outlines contain delays in resolutions of the leading tones. Dotted lines indicate some of the linear implications beyond mere triad outlines.

Melodies

The following melodies contain harmonic outlines of the I and V triads. Before singing melodies 58 through 60 make reductions on the staves provided below. Identify harmonic outlines, embellishing tones, and leading-tone resolutions.

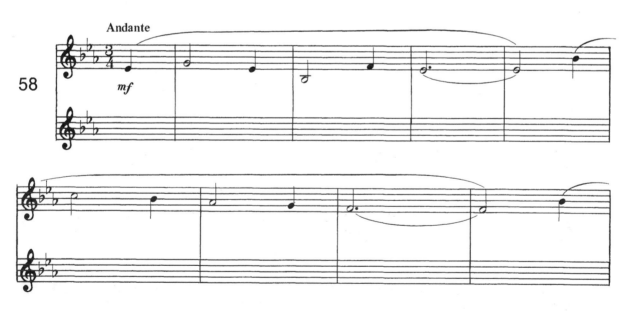

CHAPTER 4

Melodies Outlining the I and IV Triads

THE FIRST SCALE DEGREE AS A COMMON TONE

The first scale degree is common to the I and IV triad outlines in melodies (example 4.1).

Example 4.1

Other possibilities are demonstrated in example 4.2.

Example 4.2

Exercise 10

The following patterns feature the first scale degree as a pivot tone between outlines of the I and IV triads.

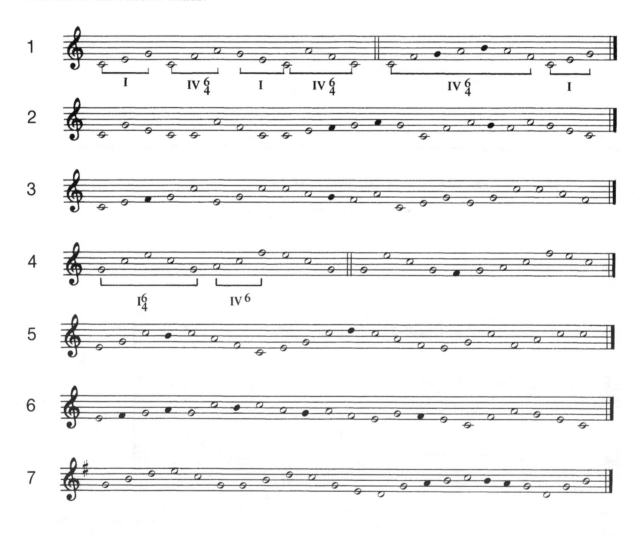

NEW RHYTHMIC MATERIAL

Typical new rhythmic patterns are summarized as follows:

An additional drill in these rhythmic patterns is found in chapter 1, rhythmic drill 5.

Melodies

The following melodies contain outlines of I and IV triads with embellishing tones. In numbers 84, 85, and 86, a reduction is given on the lower staff.

In numbers 87 through 89, space is provided for reductions.

CHAPTER 5

Melodies Outlining the I, IV and V Triads

With the introduction of the IV and V triads in chapters 3 and 4, certain tones were shown to have strong linear relationships beyond their position within individual triad outlines. Two such relationships, (1) common tones between triads and (2) leading tone resolutions, sometimes produce more than one structural level.

As stated in chapter 2, outlines of the various positions of triads produce different melodic contours, or shapes. In some of the examples and exercises in this chapter, the very contour of a melody may produce tones with linear implications that are important to hold in the mind while singing intervening tones. The reductions beneath the melody in example 5.1 reveal I, IV, and V triad outlines, plus important tones to retain in the ear while singing. Broken lines (----) have been drawn between some of those tones that suggest linear relationships beyond triad outlines.

Example 5.1

Exercise 11

This exercise contains various combinations of I, IV, and V triad outlines. Locate common tones between outlines.

NEW RHYTHMIC MATERIAL

This chapter introduces compound meters with dotted rhythms within the beat and further subdivisions of the beat. New meters are $3/8$, $4/8$, $3/16$ and $6/16$. Rhythms and meters from previous chapters continue. Typical new rhythmic patterns are summarized as follows:

Compound meters with dotted rhythms within the beat (see also chapter 1, rhythmic drill 6):

Compound meters with further subdivision of the beat (see also chapter 1, rhythmic drill 6):

New meters: $3/8$, $4/8$, $3/16$, and $6/16$ (see also chapter 1, rhythmic drill 7):

Melodies

The following melodies summarize I, IV, and V triad outlines. As a guide for retaining tonality in the ear, observe harmonic outlines and crucial pivot tones.

In numbers 113, 114, and 115, space is provided for reductions.

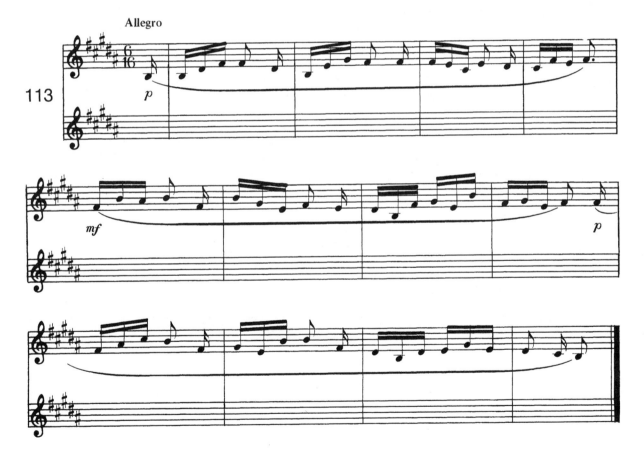

CHAPTER 6

Chromatic Variables in the Major Mode

The melodic strength of the half-step progression was discussed in relation to the leading tone (see chapters 2 and 3). A half step also lies between the third and fourth degrees of the major scale. These half steps between the seventh and eighth and the third and fourth scale degrees occur between *diatonic* tones—tones within the major scale. Half-step progressions may be produced between any other scale degrees by chromatic alteration (raising or lowering a diatonic tone with a sharp, flat, or natural sign). Some of the most common and effective chromatic alterations are those applied to embellishing tones; passing tones, neighbor tones, and appoggiaturas all have chromatic versions.

CHROMATIC NEIGHBOR TONES

The half-step chromatic neighbor tone has a stronger pull back to the decorated tone than does a whole-step neighbor tone. Compare the whole-step neighbor tone in the top staff (a) of example 6.1 with the half-step chromatic neighbor tone in the lower staff (b).

Example 6.1

Exercise 12

This exercise contains both chromatic half-step and diatonic neighbor tones.

CHROMATIC PASSING TONES

In the upper staff of example 6.2, a single passing tone fills the space between structural tones a third apart. In the lower staff, chromatic alterations create two additional tones to fill the same space.

Example 6.2

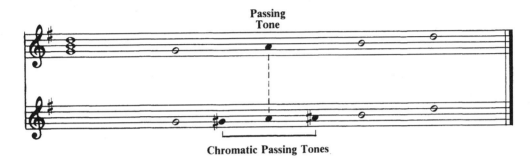

The chromatic passing tones in example 6.3 add interest and a heightened sense of motion between the structural tones G and B.

Example 6.3

In example 6.4, top staff (a), the space between F and A is filled with a single eighth-note passing tone. In the lower staff (b), the constant eighth-note motion is maintained, but the extra tones created by chromatics delay arrival of the tone A until the third beat.

Example 6.4

Analysis of such chromatic expansion is fundamental to understanding the structure of many melodies.

Chromatic passing tones in melodies allow motions not possible with diatonic passing tones. If two structural tones are one whole step apart, a chromatically altered version of one of the structural tones may serve as a passing tone between them. In example 6.5, a chromatic passing tone fills the space between structural tones G and A—one whole step apart. As with diatonic passing tones, an abundance of chromatic passing tones may obscure the underlying structure of a melody; perceptive analysis becomes even more essential.

Example 6.5

Chromatic Passing Tone

Exercise 13

The following exercise contains diatonic and chromatic neighbor tones and passing tones.

CHROMATIC APPOGGIATURAS

Similar to the other decorative tones, the appoggiatura may also have a chromatic version (compare examples 6.6 and 6.7). The structural tones to which all appoggiaturas resolve serve as guides for sight singing. In example 6.8, the F-sharp may be sung more easily if one considers its relationship to the G—the fifth of the triad.

Example 6.6

Example 6.7

Example 6.8

Exercise 14

This exercise contains typical examples of chromatic appoggiaturas. (Remember that in musical contexts appoggiaturas are found on accented beats.)

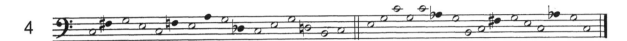

Another type of embellishing tone is the *escape tone*, or *échappée*. Each escape tone shown in example 6.9 might best be described as a neighbor tone that does not return to the decorated tone.

Example 6.9

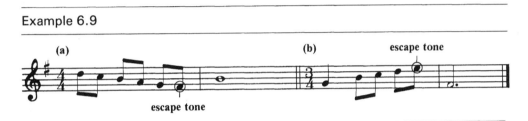

ANALYSIS OF CHROMATIC EMBELLISHING TONES

For the purpose of developing techniques in analyzing tonal melodies with chromatics, each item in exercise 15 may be sung on any of three structural levels—depending upon the singer's ability. In each item, *level a* has a pitch pattern containing triad outlines with chromatic neighbor tones, passing tones, and appoggiaturas. *Level b* contains all tones in the pattern but has differentiation between structural and decorative tones. *Level c* contains structural tones only.

Exercise 15

Sing each pattern on the level necessary for accuracy in pitch. Level a is the highest level of achievement; level c is the least challenging. When singing the chromatic appoggiaturas, utilize as tonal references the structural tones to which they progress.

1

2

3

If the following outlines cause difficulty, apply the techniques of structural analysis used above.

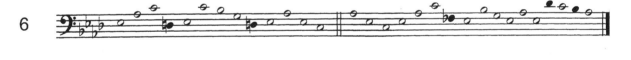

NEW RHYTHMIC MATERIAL

This chapter introduces triple division of the beat in simple meters. New meters are $^4/_2$, $^3/_2$, $^2/_2$, and $^6/_4$. Rhythms and meters from previous chapters continue. Typical new rhythmic patterns are summarized below.

Simple meters with triple division of the beat (see also chapter 1, rhythmic drill 12):

New meters: $^4/_2$, $^3/_2$, $^2/_2$, $^6/_4$ (see also chapter 1, rhythmic drill 10):

Melodies

The following melodies contain chromatics. Refer to structural levels b and c as needed.

In numbers 154 and 155, space is provided for structural analysis.

If difficulties arise in singing any of the following melodies, make reductions similar to those above.

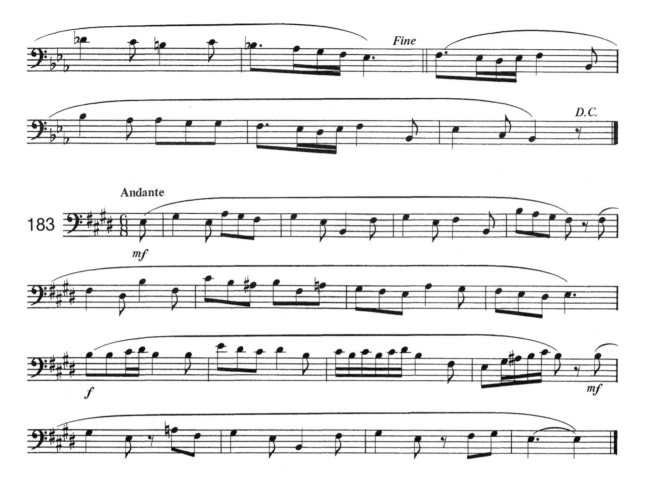

======

CHAPTER 7

Chromatic Variables in the Minor Mode

====== Chromatic embellishing tones, discussed in relation to the major mode (chapter 6), also appear in melodies in the minor mode. In addition, the sixth and seventh scale degrees are often altered chromatically in the minor mode to accommodate certain structural goals within melodies. For example, if the tonic is the immediate structural goal for a melodic passage, the seventh degree may be raised in order to function as a leading tone.

SEVENTH SCALE DEGREE AS A LEADING TONE IN MINOR

In example 7.1, the final tonic note D is interpreted as the structural goal for the passage. The raised seventh degree functions as both a lower neighbor and a leading tone to the final tonic (structural goal).

Example 7.1

D minor   Leading Tone

Exercise 16

The segments in this exercise have the raised seventh scale degree as the leading tone.

SCALE PASSAGES WITH THE TONIC AS THE STRUCTURAL GOAL

In minor scale passages involving both the sixth and seventh degrees, the sixth degree generally acts in accordance with the seventh. When the tonic is the structural goal of an ascending scale passage, both the sixth and seventh degrees are often raised (see example 7.2). If the seventh degree alone were raised in such passages, the interval of an augmented second would result between the sixth and seventh degrees. Composers of tonal music have usually avoided this augmented second by raising or lowering the sixth in accordance with the seventh.

Example 7.2

Exercise 17

This exercise involves the raised sixth and seventh in ascending scale passages with the tonic as the structural goal.

STRUCTURAL GOALS OTHER THAN THE TONIC

The seventh degree does not always function as a leading tone. If a tone other than the tonic happens to be the immediate melodic goal of a passage in the minor mode, the seventh degree is usually not raised. Example 7.3 contains an outline of the g minor triad followed by stepwise melodic motion downward to the structural goal, the dominant. As mentioned earlier, the sixth degree acts in accordance with the function of the seventh in scale passages.

Example 7.3

In example 7.4, the motion that was shown in the last four notes of example 7.3 is expanded by prolongation of the tones G and E-flat. The seventh degree is raised and then lowered according to its changing functions: (a) a raised lower neighbor and leading tone to the tonic, (b) an unaltered passing tone in the overall motion from tonic to dominant, and (c) an unaltered upper neighbor tone to the E-flat. As with any attempts to formulate general rules about music, however, exceptions to

Example 7.4

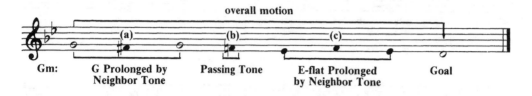

the altered sixth and seventh degrees may be found. In actual melodies, there may be interpretations of tones based on criteria other than chord outlines. Example 7.5 contains a melodic fragment in which the sixth and seventh degrees have separate functions. The sixth acts as an upper neighbor to the C-sharp (dominant) and remains unaltered; the seventh is a raised leading tone which eventually resolves to the tonic. Example 7.6 has the identical pitches of example 7.5, but with a new rhythmic setting which gives prominence to the D (sixth degree).

Example 7.5

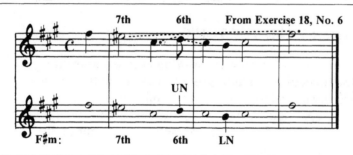

Example 7.6

The rhythmic prominence of the D in example 7.6 allows it to be raised along with the seventh degree in the ultimate resolution to the F-sharp (tonic).

Exercise 18

The following exercise contains a mixture of tonic and dominant goals. As in examples from earlier chapters, the structural tones may be obscured by embellishing tones. Study each item before singing it.

Numbers 6 and 7 have delays in the resolution of the leading tone.

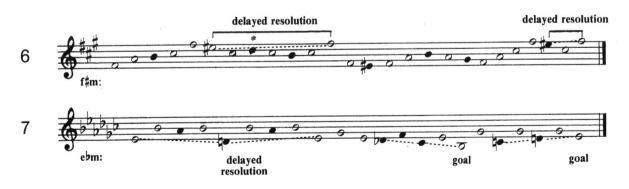

_____

*The D (sixth degree) functions as an upper neighbor to the C-sharp. Depending upon rhythmic placement and duration, the D may be raised and therefore be interpreted as belonging with the leading tone in its eventual resolution to the tonic.

NEW RHYTHMIC MATERIAL

Typical new rhythmic patterns are summarized as follows.

Syncopation (see also chapter 1, rhythmic drill 8):

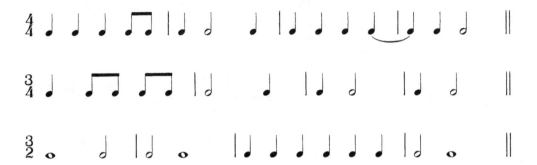

Melodies

The following melodies in minor keys include chromatic embellishing tones, plus variable sixth and seventh scale degrees.

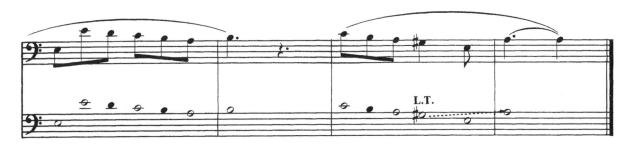

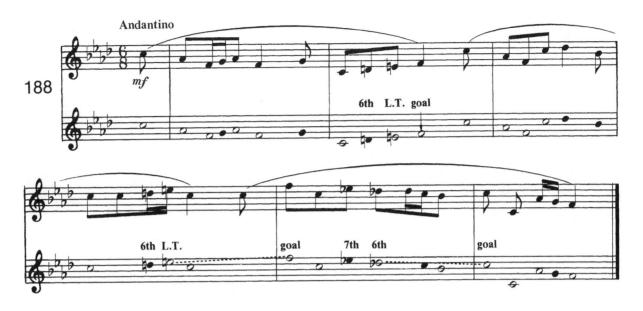

In numbers 189 through 192, space is provided for analysis.

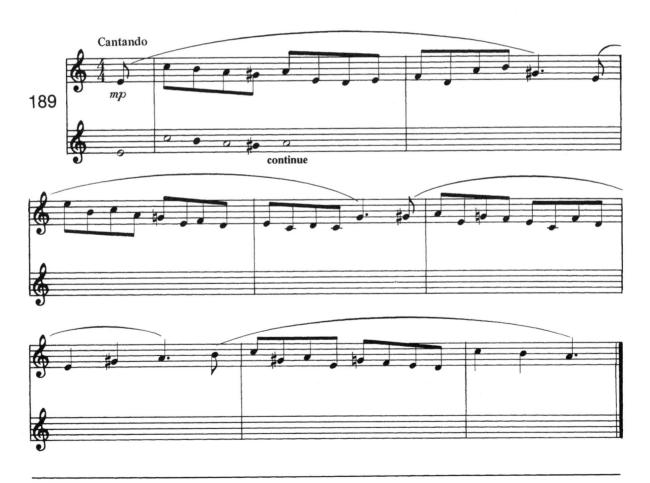

If difficulties arise in singing any of the following melodies, make reductions similar to those above.

CHAPTER 8

Melodies Outlining the Dominant Seventh Chord

$\mathbf{A}$ dominant seventh chord may be constructed by adding a minor third above a dominant (V) chord. In the key of C major, the V chord (G-B-D) becomes a V^7 if the tone F is added. The F is a seventh above the root of the chord (see example 8.1).

Example 8.1

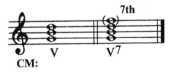

Melodic outlines of the V^7 and V chords are similar; each has a common tone with the I triad, and each contains the leading tone with its tendency to pull toward the tonic.

Exercise 19

The following harmonic outlines contain common tones between the I and V^7 chords.

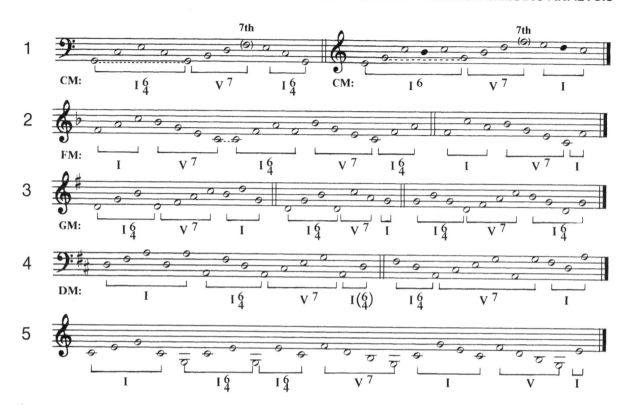

___

RESOLUTION OF THE SEVENTH IN THE V⁷ CHORD

The seventh of the V^7 chord (fourth scale degree) generally resolves downward to the third of the scale (third of the tonic triad). (See exercise 20.)

Exercise 20

Note resolutions of the seventh in the following V^7 chord outlines.

The fourth scale degree is common to both the IV and V^7 chords (see example 8.2). Melodic patterns may involve the common tone between the IV triad and the V^7 chord.

Example 8.2

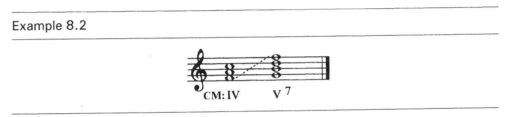

Exercise 21

The following patterns are outlines of I, IV, V, and V^7 chords. Note common tones and resolutions of the seventh.

DELAYED RESOLUTION OF THE SEVENTH

Resolution of the seventh in the V^7 chord may be obscured by a delay. In a delayed resolution, the seventh resolves only after intervening tones are sung (see also Delay of Leading-Tone Resolution, chapter 3). In example 8.3, separate forces on two structural levels compete for attention: (a) the delayed resolution of the seventh and (b) the motion between the last two notes in the example. In such passages, mistakes may occur if the singer ignores the underlying structural levels and concentrates solely on note-to-note progressions. The patterns in example 8.3 call for structural analysis and tonal memory. If the eventual resolution of the seventh is anticipated and held in the memory while singing the intervening tones, the final tone E may be sung as a result of this resolution rather than as simply a major sixth above the preceding G.

Example 8.3

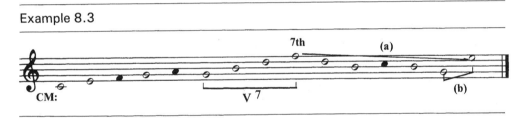

The reduction beneath the melody in example 8.4 shows not only harmonic outlines but also a delayed resolution of the seventh of the V^7 chord outline. Examine the reduction carefully before singing. Notice that the final tone completes the resolution of the seventh. Sing the fragment but stop immediately at point x. Try to recall the seventh. If the seventh has not been retained in the memory, begin again and stop at x once more. When the seventh can be recalled, finish the excerpt.

Example 8.4

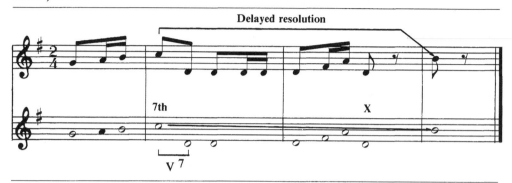

Since many melodies contain structural levels similar to those demonstrated in examples 8.3 and 8.4, the ability to analyze and interpret these levels is essential for improving tonal memory and sight-singing ability. Tonal memory becomes the tool for developing sight-singing skill.

Chord outlines may sometimes be obscured by embellishing tones and delayed resolutions of the seventh. In some cases, large intervals are created because of missing harmonic tones. The singer may wish to supply the missing tones mentally as an aid in singing the patterns. In certain contexts the interval of a seventh may result from an embellishing tone within a tonic triad outline. Compare (a) and (b) in example 8.5. The next chapter will deal more extensively with techniques for singing large intervals through considerations of melodic contours.

Example 8.5

Exercise 22

Harmonic outlines in this exercise summarize contours of the I, IV, V, and V⁷ chords. Note resolutions of the seventh of the V⁷ and the leap of a seventh within harmonic outlines. A few linear contours are indicated with dotted lines; draw others if needed.

NEW RHYTHMIC MATERIAL

Typical new rhythmic patterns are summarized as follows:

Syncopation within the beat (see also chapter 1, rhythmic drill 9):

Hemiola (see also chapter 1, rhythmic drill 16):

Melodies

The following melodies contain outlines of I, IV, V, and V⁷ chords. Note resolutions of the seventh.

In numbers 229 through 232, space is provided for analysis on the staff below.

CHAPTER 9

Melodic Contours

Material in the preceding chapters develops sight-singing skill through analysis of structural and decorative tones within harmonic outlines in melodies. Beginning with this chapter, analysis will go beyond the limitations of treating only harmonic outlines; general linear contours involving entire phrases will be considered as well.

THE V⁷ CHORD OUTLINE AND MELODIC CONTOUR

In the previous chapters, intervals as large as a major sixth were encountered in outlines of inverted triads. In chapter 8, the interval of a seventh resulted from leaps within outlines of the V⁷ chord. The expansion of melodic analysis to include larger intervals and broader melodic contours is facilitated by further considerations of the familiar V⁷ chord outline.

The melody in level a of example 9.1 outlines I, IV, and V⁷ chords. The reduction in level b distinguishes between harmonic tones and embellishing tones. In addition, level b is supplied with dotted lines to suggest overall linear patterns not implied in a strict consideration of harmonic outlines. These overall patterns, or contours, offer more general points of reference for the ear than mere note-to-note progressions. The reduction in level c omits embellishing tones. Perhaps for ease in sight singing, level c should be attempted first.

When singing level c, note that frequent reversals of the motion between upper and lower registers tend to create two distinct melodic curves. Tones connected with one dotted line should be retained in the ear while singing intervening tones in the other line.

After singing level c successfully, sing level b. With the melodic line in level b somewhat obscured by embellishing tones, it may be useful to try remembering the tone at x as a reference for later singing the tone at point y. The structural implication of point z (under the bracket) is the delayed resolution of the seventh of the dominant seventh chord.

Example 9.1

When levels c and b have been mastered, sing the original melody in level a. The above procedure utilizes tonal memory as an aid in anticipating the successions of tones in melodic patterns.

Thus far in this study all embellishing tones, regardless of metric placement or accent, have been understood within the context of harmonic outlines. For example, the appoggiatura is a leap to a tone above or below a harmonic tone and, in spite of its usual placement on a strong beat or fraction of a beat, is understood in terms of its origin and eventual resolution to a harmonic tone. In analyzing melodies for overall contour, meter and rhythmic accent must also be taken into account, since these factors might project certain tones into prominence and thus into the memory. In example 9.1, the tone B (point x in level b) is an important structural reference because of its harmonic function and rhythmic position. However, when the first 16 pitches of example 9.1 are given a new set of durations in example 9.2, the tone B seems less significant for tonal memory due to its relatively short duration. Instead, the new rhythmic pattern seems to project the tone D into a more prominent role. Because of its longer duration and location on a strong beat, the tone D then becomes the logical tone to remember in singing from point x to point y.

Example 9.2

Melodies

Before singing numbers 273, 274, and 275, note the harmonic outlines in level b and the contours in level c.

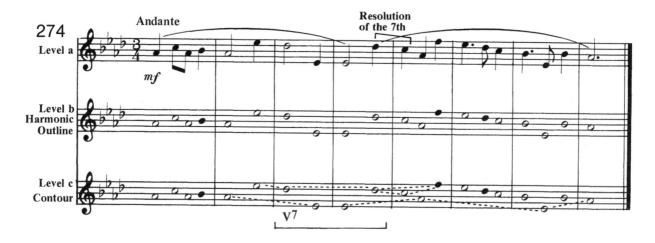

In numbers 276 and 277, space is provided for analysis of harmonic outlines and melodic contours.

RISING AND FALLING MELODIC CONTOURS

A melodic curve with a rising and falling motion inevitably has important correspondences between tones of its ascending and descending segments.

Exercise 23

In singing the following patterns, retain the appropriate tones in the ear as references.

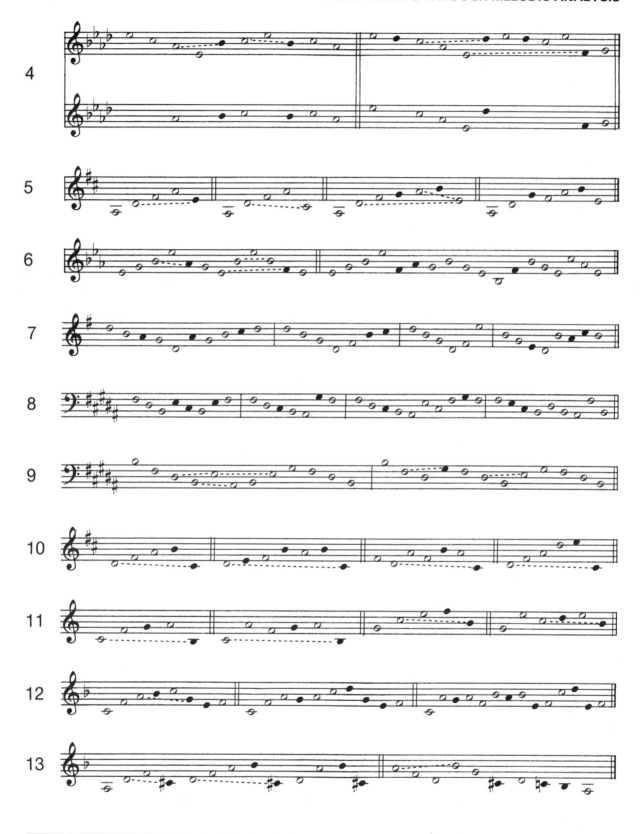

Melodies

Correspondences between rising and falling segments of each melody are shown in the partial reductions in the lower staff.

In numbers 297 and 298, space is provided for reductions.

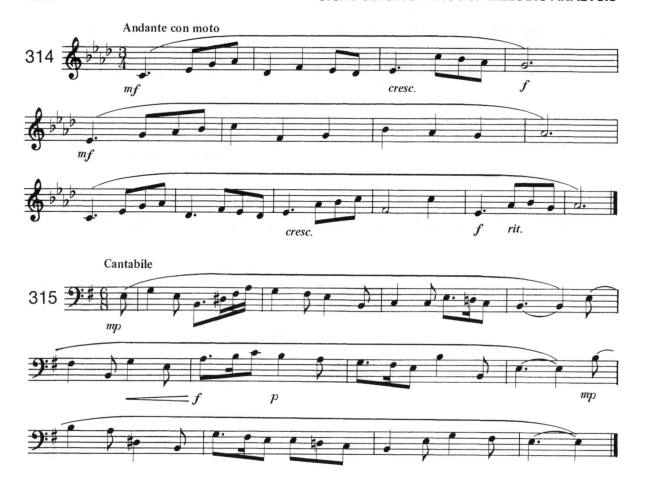

SCALEWISE MELODIC CONTOURS

Some melodies have underlying scalewise patterns that are obscured by intervening tones. In example 9.3, the analysis on the lower staff reveals a second structural level consisting of a descending scalewise pattern. As in previous sections, tonal memory is essential in sight singing.

Example 9.3

Melodies

Numbers 316 through 325 contain underlying scalewise passages.

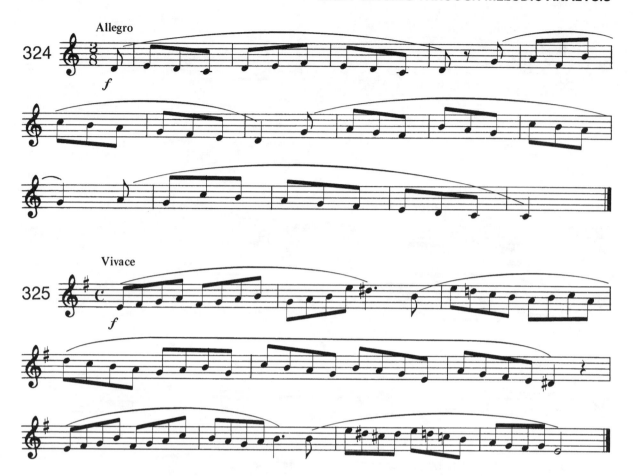

CHAPTER 10

Melodic Contours: Two Melodies in One

A melody may have a contour that is the result of frequent alternations between pitches in upper and lower registers. At first glance, the melody in example 10.1 (level a) seems to contain merely a series of large intervals (level b). However, closer analysis reveals two distinct underlying melodic contours (level c). Before attempting to sing from note to note through the series of intervals in level b, examine the two-part implications in level c. Sing the upper part (indicated with a dotted line in level c) and then the lower part. Next, practice combining the two lines into a single melodic pattern. In singing such a pattern, a tone in one line should be retained in the ear while singing any intervening tones in the opposite line. The skill involved here is *tonal memory*.

Example 10.1

Exercise 24

In the following two-in-one melodic outlines, sing each implied line separately. Then, using tonal memory, connect the two lines into a single series of tones.

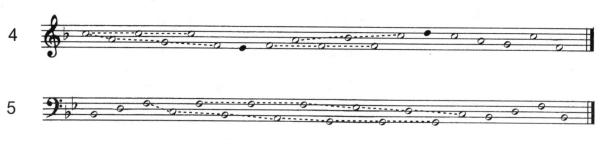

In each of the two-in-one outlines in numbers 4 through 6, one part remains stationary while the other part moves.

In numbers 7 through 9, the parts of the two-in-one outlines move in parallel motion—at the interval of a sixth.

As with other patterns, two-in-one outlines may be obscured by embellishing tones as well as relatively lengthy distances between structural tones. The two-in-one outlines in numbers 10 through 13 are obscured by embellishing tones.

Although two-part (two-in-one) melodic outlines are generally associated with the music of Bach and other baroque composers, examination reveals that at least partial two-part outlines are common in melodies from a variety of styles and periods. Scanning a melody for two-part outlines often clarifies an entire passage that appears on the surface to be a series of difficult intervals.

Exercise 25

The following patterns contain two-part outlines as well as harmonic outlines studied in previous chapters.

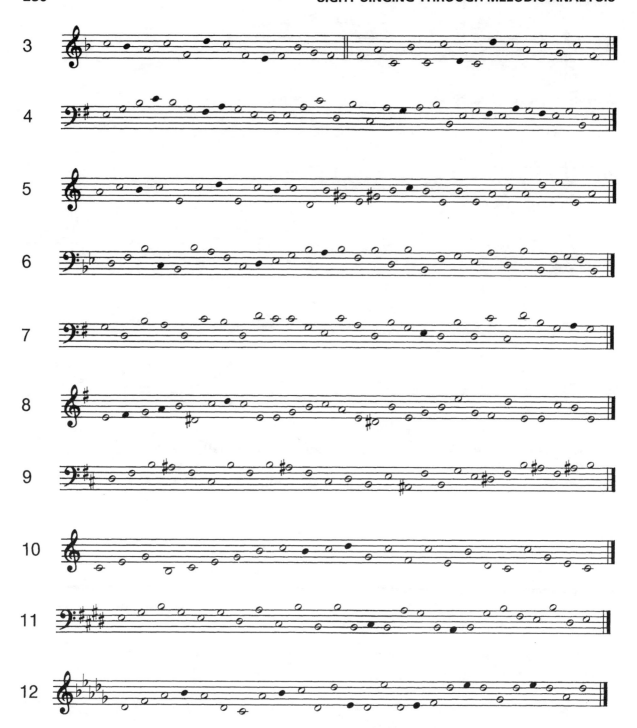

Numbers 13 through 22 contain diatonic and chromatic passing tones, neighbor tones, and appoggiaturas within two-part melodic contours.

INTRODUCTION OF TENOR AND ALTO CLEFS

Melodies

The following melodies have two-part outlines. Tenor and alto clefs are included. In numbers 326, 327, and 328 the underlying two-part outlines and other significant structural implications are shown in the reductions.

In numbers 329 through 332, space is provided for analysis on the staff below.

CHAPTER 11

Melodies with Modulation

Many melodies in music literature contain changes in key, or *modulation*. The most common modulation in major keys is the one from the tonic to the dominant. In shorter melodies, a brief shift of tonality to the dominant triad outline may just as well be interpreted as a mere prolongation of the dominant of the original key. If, however, the dominant is confirmed by reiteration of its own dominant and occupies a relatively lengthy portion of the overall melody, perhaps one should consider that a key change has been achieved. Once a modulation has been established, all tones should assume their proper relationships within the new key.

MODULATION TO THE DOMINANT

In the scanning of a melody for sight singing, appearances of the raised fourth scale degree may signal a modulation to the dominant. The raised fourth degree may function as a leading tone and thus imply the dominant triad of the new key. Only a sufficient duration of the new tonal level will confirm a modulation.

In the first melodic outline in exercise 26, the notes indicated by the bracket are a prolongation of the dominant rather than a modulation. The shift to the dominant is of short duration with respect to overall length, and harmonies closely related to the dominant are not present to reinforce a new tonality.

Exercise 26

Analyze each of the following patterns before singing. Remember that the raised fourth scale degree is sometimes a clue to a modulation to the dominant. Numbers 2, 3, and 4 contain modulations to the dominant.

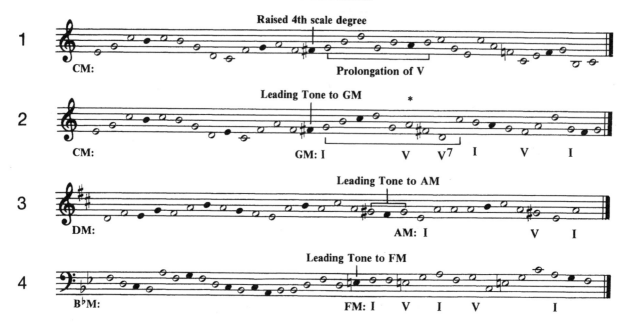

Before singing the following, analyze each for possible modulations.

*The D-major triad, dominant of G major, aids in establishing G major as the new tonality.

9

Melodies

The following melodies may contain modulations. Analyze each and sing.

D.C. al Fine

MODULATION BETWEEN RELATIVE MAJOR AND MINOR KEYS

Modulation between relative keys occurs frequently in music literature. Due to the common triads between relative keys, such modulations are smooth and practically imperceptible to untrained ears. One chromatic tone, the leading tone in the minor scale, may serve as a clue to a possible modulation between relative keys. The disappearance of the raised leading tone in a minor key may mean that a modulation to its relative major is in progress (see example 11.1). Conversely, an appearance of the raised fifth scale degree in a major key may signal a modulation to its relative minor (see example 11.2). Other reasons for the inclusion or exclusion of raised leading tones and other chromatics are discussed elsewhere. (See chapter 6 on chromatic embellishing tones and chapter 7 for variable sixth and seventh scale degrees in minor.)

Example 11.1

Example 11.2

Exercise 27

The following patterns involve modulations between relative major and minor keys.

Melodies

The following melodies contain modulations between relative major and minor keys. Observe the chromatics involved in each modulation.

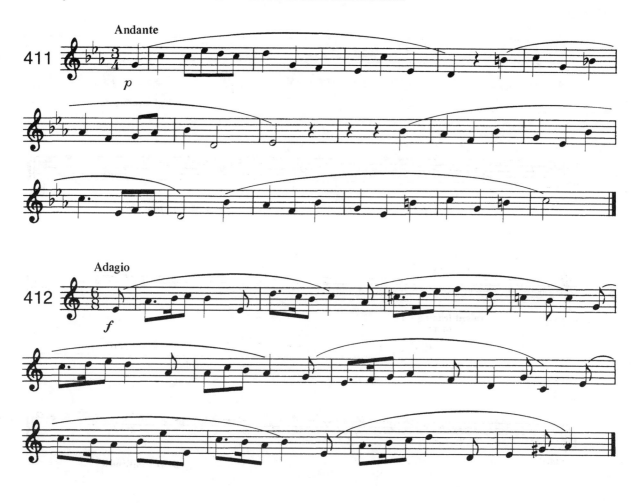

Numbers 421 through 438 have modulations without chromatics.

Numbers 439 through 449 have modulations to tonalities other than the dominant
or relative key.

CHAPTER 12
======

Modal Melodies

T he major and minor modes are only two of the modes that are an integral part of musical composition in a variety of styles. In this chapter each melody will be in one of six modes: *Ionian, Dorian, Phrygian, Lydian, Mixolydian,* or *Aeolian.* Each of these modes is identifiable by its unique arrangement of whole and half steps. As may be seen in example 12.1, the Ionian and Aeolian correspond to the major and relative minor scales, respectively.

The piano keyboard serves as a good visual reference for determining the patterns of the modes. Excluding all black keys on the keyboard, the Ionian mode (major scale) results if one plays from C to C. The half steps are between the third and fourth, and seventh and eighth scale degrees. The pattern of the Dorian mode is revealed if one plays from D to D on the white keys only; half steps are between the second and third, and the sixth and seventh scale degrees. The Phrygian mode lies between E and E, the Lydian between F and F, the Mixolydian between G and G, and the Aeolian (natural minor) between A and A.

Example 12.1

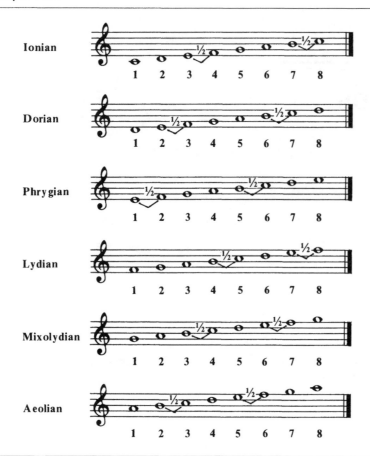

Although each mode in example 12.1 is shown on the tonal level at which no key signature is required, each pattern may be transposed to other levels as well. If the Dorian mode were transposed to F, for example, accidentals or a key signature of three flats (B-flat, E-flat, and A-flat) would be required in order to construct the pattern (see example 12.2). Likewise, all the modes would require accidentals or key signatures for transpositions to tonal levels other than those shown in example 12.1. As with tonal melodies in previous chapters, modal melodies may also have chromatic embellishing tones.

Example 12.2

Melodies

Before singing each of the following melodies, determine the mode.

CHAPTER 13

Melodies Containing either Complex Tonal or Complex Rhythmic Patterns

M elodies in this chapter are grouped into two broad catego-
ries: (1) extensive chromatics with moderately difficult rhythmic patterns and meters and (2) moderately difficult pitch patterns with complex rhythm and meters.
Under the first category, melodies are further grouped into extensive chromatics
within triad outlines, large intervals with chromatics, familiar patterns with enharmonic spellings, and nontriadic melodies (whole-tone patterns and melodies
based upon quartal and quintal harmonies).

EXTENSIVE CHROMATICS WITH MODERATELY DIFFICULT RHYTHMIC PATTERNS AND METERS

Extensive Chromatics within Triad Outlines

The melodies in this section have extensive chromatics associated with underlying harmonic outlines. Without careful analysis, such outlines may not be appar-
ent. Although many of the chromatic tones in these melodies may not adhere to
their expected tendencies to resolve, the singer may still relate these tones to famil-

iar harmonic outlines. In example 13.1, the reduction demonstrates how the tone A-flat, although it lacks a resolution, may be related to the C-major triad.

Example 13.1

Large Intervals with Chromatics

Reading melodies containing intervals greater than an octave is often facilitated by mentally placing all notes within the range of the octave. In example 13.2, notes in the rather angular melodic line have been reduced in the staff below to a much more manageable line within an octave. In performing the melody, the singer may wish to consider the reduced version first and then approach the original melody as merely involving displacement of some notes by the interval of an octave.

Example 13.2

Familiar Patterns with Enharmonic Spellings

Some chromatic passages may be performed more easily if the singer relates certain chromatic pitches enharmonically to familiar patterns. In example 13.3, the pitches in brackets clearly outline enharmonically an A-flat major triad in first inversion. It should be understood, however, that such enharmonic associations are merely an aid in singing the patterns; no attempt should be made to interpret the tones within the bracket as an actual A-flat major triad.

Example 13.3

Nontriadic Melodies

Melodies based on quartal harmony (chords built in fourths instead of thirds) may contain patterns in which the interval of a fourth is prominent. At first, such melodies may not seem to lend themselves to comparison with triad outlines. However, there are some possibilities for relating melodies based on fourths to more familiar triad or interval patterns. The melody in example 13.4 is composed almost entirely of the interval of a fourth. Below the melody are alternative suggestions for relating to more familiar underlying patterns. If such comparative patterns are useful for singing melodies, the singer should not hesitate to construct these "artificial" guides.

Example 13.4

Melodies

The following melodies contain extensive chromatics with moderately difficult meters and rhythm. Numbers 498 through 518 have extensive chromatics within triad outlines. Reductions are provided in numbers 498 through 500.

Numbers 519 through 525 have large intervals with chromatics.

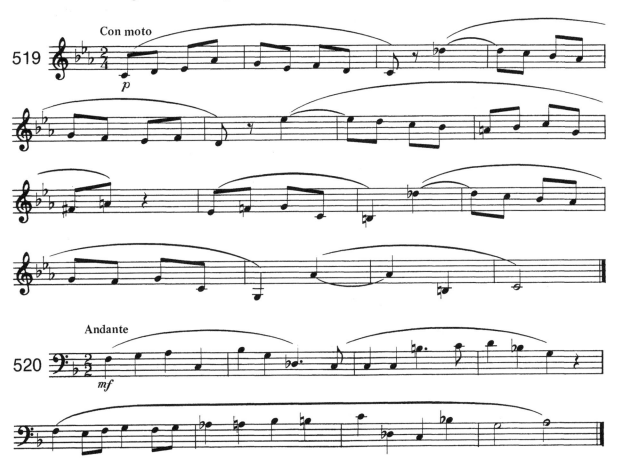

Numbers 526 through 529 have familiar patterns with enharmonic spellings.

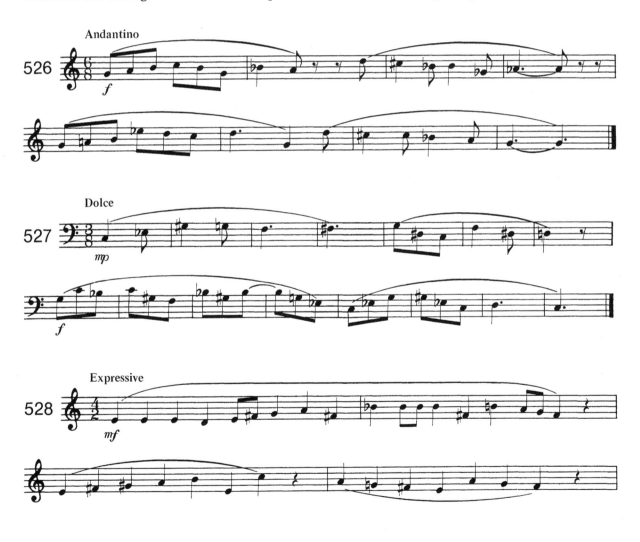

Numbers 530 through 535 have nontriadic melodies (whole-tone patterns and melodies based upon quartal and quintal harmonies).

MODERATELY DIFFICULT PITCH PATTERNS WITH COMPLEX RHYTHM AND METERS

Melodies in this section have pitch patterns of only moderate difficulty, while new meters and rhythmic patterns are more challenging. If any of the remaining pitch patterns should present difficulties, the singer is encouraged to make reductions similar to those in previous sections.

New Rhythmic Material

Typical new meters and rhythmic patterns are summarized as follows:

See also chapter 1, rhythmic drills 11, 13, 14, 15, 17, and 18.

Melodies

The following melodies have moderately difficult pitch patterns with complex rhythms and meters.

Quickly

536

CHAPTER 14

Melodies Containing Both Complex Tonal and Complex Rhythmic Patterns

Melodies in this chapter summarize the tonal and rhythmic material in chapter 13. Both difficult pitch patterns and complex rhythms may be incorporated into the same melody. If the tonal material of any of the following melodies presents difficulty, the singer is encouraged to make reductions similar to those in previous chapters.

Melodies

The following melodies contain both complex tonal and complex rhythmic patterns.